A BOOK OF BELIEFS

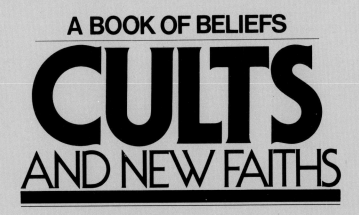

CULTS
AND NEW FAITHS

JOHN BUTTERWORTH

David C. Cook Publishing Co.
ELGIN, ILLINOIS—WESTON, ONTARIO

To Jan

Published in the United States by
David C. Cook Publishing Co.
850 N. Grove, Elgin, IL 60120
ISBN: 0 89191 479 X

Library of Congress Catalog Card No. LC 81–67763
All rights reserved.
First United States edition 1981

Published in the United Kingdom by
Lion Publishing
Icknield Way, Tring, Herts, England
ISBN: 0 85648 249 8

Published in Australia by
Albatross Books
PO Box 320, Sutherland, NSW 2232, Australia
ISBN: 0 86760 259 7

First edition 1981

Printed by New Interlitho SPA, Italy

The photographs in this book are reproduced by
permission of the following photographers and
organizations:
Associated Press 30–31(both)
Barnaby's Picture Library 23, 24–25
Bisonte Archive 57(right)
Camera Press 4–5, 10-11, 28, 38–39
E. J. Cardell 46–47(above all)
Mary Evans Picture Library 16, 17, 48–49(all)
Philip Hainsworth 44–45(all), 46–47(below)
Keystone Press 12–13(below), 19, 20–21, 38(left),
54(left), 56–57, 60–61
Peter Langford 26(picture in brooch)
Lion Publishing: Jon Willcocks cover, title pages, 2–3,
8(below), 9(above), 14–15, 26–27, 40–41, 50–51, 58–59
Mansell Collection 8(above), 32–33(below)
Polydor Records 27, 35(right)
Popperfoto 6–7, 32(above), 36, 37
Radio Times Hulton Picture Library 9(below), 34–35
David Redfern 54–55
Syndication International 12(above), 22
John Topham Picture Library 18

CONTENTS

CULTS
AND NEW FAITHS

CULTS AND NEW FAITHS

'May I come in and discuss the Bible with you?'

'Would you like to buy a candle to help missionary work?'

'May I talk to you about your life?'

At one time or another, everyone has been approached and asked these sort of questions. And most people do not know how to react. Is this a visit from the church I went to last Christmas? Is it another charity collection? Or is it some new cult I have read about in the paper?

In the last 100 years, and especially since the 1960s, the increase in new religions, cults and faiths has been enormous. Many of the followers are in their teens or early twenties. But they also come from all ages and backgrounds. They range from the conservatively-dressed, studious Mormons to the orange-robed, shaven-headed followers of the eastern Hare Krishna movement.

But how can we tell what the movements are like? Most people used to dismiss them as small groups of cranks who were best left alone. But since the tragic mass suicide of the Jonestown People's Temple in Guyana, and TV coverage of brainwashing techniques in other cults, people have begun to realize the dangers such groups can represent.

Jesus told his followers: 'Beware of false prophets who come to you in sheep's clothing but inwardly are ravenous wolves.' As in Jesus' day, so today we have a real problem with 'false prophets'.

Who are they?

New groups which attract the label 'cults' often have certain characteristics. They frequently have a very strong, charismatic leader. Absolute obedience to the leader and his teaching is often called for. This obedience can include giving up home, job, family and possessions.

There seem to be four main categories of cult. There are the **self-improvement groups** such as Scientology, whose members are trying to discover themselves and improve their personalities. There are the **eastern groups** such as the Divine Light Mission, whose followers believe that the mystical East gives more meaning to life than the materialistic West. There are the **unification groups** such as the Moonies, who take elements of truth from many religions and claim to fulfil them all. There are the **Christian deviation groups** such as the Children of God and The Way, which seem to have been genuinely Christian to begin with but put so much emphasis on their own added teachings that they can no longer be called so.

Other new (and not-so-new) faiths cannot be labelled as cults. Baha'i, for example, is a prime example of a unification group, but is much more a young religion than a cult. Christadelphianism, Seventh-Day Adventism and Moral Re-Armament are movements which have sprung from mainstream Christianity and have their own distinctive teachings.

Why the growth in cults?

Many people, particularly the young, are thoroughly dissatisfied with society. Politics provides no answers. Science creates more problems than it solves. Mechanistic views of man and society have made man impersonal and in need of a true identity.

The future seems frightening, with the threat

of nuclear war and the running down of natural resources. At the same time family life is providing no security and the church in the West seems to be declining.

People are looking for help. And in many cases the cults seem to offer it. They have a highly organized system to believe in and become involved with. They show real interest in welcoming new members and a real enthusiasm for spreading their message.

What can be done?

By and large, members of the cults are sincere people who feel that they have discovered something important. If you speak to them on the street corner you will find most of them friendly enough—though rather persistent in their conversation. Most street-level members genuinely feel that they are right in their beliefs.

But, unfortunately, many members have found out only too late that what they have become involved with has hidden undercurrents, which they are less than happy about. It can be very hard for a member to do anything about this when he is surrounded by the pressure of a close-knit group. Can anything be done to help?

First, the facts should be made known. In some cases we do not have to look far before we see danger signs. In others pitfalls are there, but carefully hidden. Jesus said, 'You will know them by their fruit'. As a journalist and a Christian I hope that the following pages will help to show up those of them which are 'false prophets' by showing something of their 'fruit'. In short articles such as these, it has been impossible to go into great detail—and often the facts are changing very rapidly.

Second, those who are vulnerable should be helped—young people, the mentally handicapped, the lonely, the drifters, the bereaved. We should help them to see the possible dangers involved.

Most of all, the real answers should be examined, both to spiritual needs and to the problems of society. The answers of mainstream Christianity are as relevant today as ever, with the appeal of Jesus Christ for us to come to him and find new life.

KEY QUESTIONS

If you want to find out whether a group is in the mainstream of Christian teaching you can do so by asking three questions.

Who was Jesus? Christians believe that Jesus was a real historical figure and that he was both God and man. Most heresies deny at least one of these points.

How can man be saved? The Bible states: 'By grace you have been saved through faith; and this is not your own doing, it is the gift of God—not because of works lest any man should boast.' False prophets emphasize in one way or another that man can earn his way to heaven by doing the right things.

What is their authority? Christians accept the Bible as their supreme authority and as God's revelation to man. Many false prophets use additional 'revelations' which they make equal with the Bible as 'God's revelation for the present age'. Others accept the authority of the Bible—but only as interpreted by their leader.

THE CHILDREN OF GOD

"Drop out of the system and live for Jesus: Judgement is coming soon."

'We are revolutionary Christian nomads, bypassing the hopeless, unresponsive older generation and churchy people and bringing new-time religion to a New Generation,' claim the Children of God. The movement, which was begun in 1968 by David Brandt Berg, claims to have 2 million converts and 8,000 missionaries worldwide. Followers hand over all their possessions to the movement and live in colonies, in order to 'return to the truth, love, peace and beauty of our ancients . . . the simple life of true happiness in God and love for our fellow man'.

Revolutionary beginnings

In 1969 David Berg claimed that he had received a prophecy from God: an earthquake would send California crashing into the sea and he, like Moses, would lead God's children through the desert.

Berg was born in 1919, the son of an evangelist couple, and for a time he was a pastor of the Christian and Missionary Alliance church. But he fell out with the leaders and became disillusioned with institutionalized religion. He moved to Huntington Beach, California, where he began working with drop-outs. One hundred and fifty of them followed 'Moses David', or 'Mo' as he was known, out of California on their journey into the desert.

For several months they wandered around witnessing, until TV evangelist Fred Jordan allowed them to stay at his 400-acre ranch in Texas. They used his ranch as the base from which to prepare the world for Jesus' Second Coming. In return they appeared on Jordan's TV show. But in 1971 Jordan evicted them after a row and they set up colonies, first in America and then throughout the world.

Very little is known about Moses David, who refuses to be interviewed. He is believed to live in Europe, probably in Italy, in self-imposed seclusion, having delegated most of the day-to-day running of the movement to trusted deputies.

Life as a Child of God

The Children of God expect a Communist takeover of the West, leading to persecution of Christians. They say the best way to prepare for

this is to live as though it has already happened. So followers live in colonies, some of which are surrounded by 'No Trespassing' signs and high cyclone fences.

To join the movement a person has to sign a form saying: 'I promise to give all my goods and income, to let you open my mail. I will obey rules and officers.' A new member goes first to a 'babe's colony'. Early in the movement's history, new members spent up to eight hours a day in Bible study and memorized hundreds of Bible verses. Today that emphasis has changed. After the babe's colony he will join another colony of about 12 people. The word 'commune' is not used, since it has connotations of sexual permissiveness. A member, who will often adopt a new biblical name, will rarely have a day off and will have no privacy, as otherwise Satan might tempt him.

The main task of the members is to sell literature on the streets. Members who achieve their quota are 'shiners', and are rewarded with a little money for their own use. Those who fail are 'shamers' and have to do extra jobs such as washing up or cleaning the toilets. Regular 'shamers' are sent to a town without a colony where they have to raise enough money to pay for their own board and keep for a month.

In its early days in America, the Children of God picked up many followers from the confused and chaotic youth culture of cities such as Los Angeles. The group offered the young disciples emotional security and a revolutionary message.

KEY BELIEFS

● They are the only true followers of God.

● The world-system, including schools, governments, churches and families, is inspired by the Devil.

● Moses David is God's prophet for today.

● No action is wrong in itself. Everything depends on attitude. If a deed is done 'in the spirit', it is right. If it is done 'in the flesh', it is wrong.

● Jesus will return to earth in 1993.

● Before then the Children of God will preach to the whole world. They will be helped in this by Colonel Gadaffi of Libya, who will make peace with Israel.

● The Battle of Armageddon will take place when Russia invades Israel. America will be drawn into the conflict and, along with Israel, be decisively beaten. A world Communist government will then be set up and will last for seven years until Jesus returns.

The changing teaching

In the last few years the Children of God, or the Family of Love as they now like to be known, has changed radically. The emphasis on the movement used to be on Jesus—now it is on Moses David. An ex-follower, whose wife was one of the movement's founder members in Huntington Beach said: 'Having a confrontation with Christ isn't the big thing any more. The key to success in COG is how effectively a person fits into the Moses David witnessing machine, producing more income and more disciples for King David.'

In the early days, followers were taught from the Bible. Now, however, the teaching is based on the MO letters. The movement's two main Bible teachers, Joab and Joel Wordsworth, have been denounced by Moses David and excommunicated. Berg has warned all members to destroy Joel's letters, threatening them with excommunication if they do not.

And the inspiration of the MO letters has become very dubious, as Moses David has become more and more involved in the occult. He claims to have a number of 'spiritual counsellors' who give him revelations, supposedly from God. They include Rasputin, the Pied Piper, Joan of Arc, Oliver Cromwell, Merlin the Magician and Martin Luther. His main counsellor is Abrahim, a supposed gypsy king who died a thousand years ago. Abrahim's messages include much that is heretical and blasphemous.

The changing practices

Even more sensational is Moses David's claim that he has sex with spirits, whom he calls goddesses. The whole movement has become increasingly sex-orientated. Moses David wrote: 'We have a sexy God and a sexy religion and a very sexy leader with a very sexy following. So if you don't like sex you had better get out while you can.' Now women followers are expected to go out onto the streets and become 'hookers for Jesus'—religious prostitutes.

In FFers Handbook (FF stands for 'flirty fish') Moses David tells women: 'There's no reason not to display the blessing of the Lord ... Don't be afraid to wear low-cut gowns with very low necklines even to the waist or navel—no bras, see-through blouses. Show them what you've got— that's the bait ... I want them to absolutely totally flip and fall in love with you.'

The point, says Moses David, is that 'in one night you can show what a love slave you are and how sweet and humble and unselfish you are ... You'd better let them understand from the beginning that the reason you love them so much, that you're willing to give them everything, is because God loves them so much and expects them to give Him everything in return'.

The changing movement

In a magazine article in 1977, David Jacks, a former Children of God archbishop, explained why he had left the movement, and why he believed Berg to be a false prophet: 'I am convinced that in the early days most members really received Jesus as their personal saviour when they entered the group ... But now the Children of God is degenerating. David Berg is getting more and more into pornography, spiritism, astrology and other far-out things—substituting this garbage for the fundamental Christian faith.'

In the early 70s, the European headquarters of the Children of God was this converted warehouse in south London. Here disciples lived in community and planned their outreach.

The main way in which Moses David communicates with his followers, most of whom have never seen him, is by the 'MO letter'. These letters contain his teachings and his latest revelations concerning future world events, which he claims to receive in a trance from his spirit guides. Some of the MO letters are sold to the public and bring in as much as $1 million profit a month.

Moses David wrote his first MO letter, *The Old Church and the New Church*, to get himself out of a tight spot. Word was getting out that he had left his wife and was living with his secretary. In the letter he explained that his wife represented the old church and his secretary the new. God was putting away the old, which was a hindrance.

Since then he has written many hundreds of letters, including the pornographic *In the beginning—Sex* and *Come on Ma! Burn your Bra*. In one letter, *God bless you and Goodbye*, he even confessed that he was a false prophet, but this was quickly followed by another letter which claimed that the previous one was a forgery.

ARE THEY THE CHILDREN OF GOD?

● The New Testament shows that the early church's 'commune' was temporary and voluntary. The Children of God say that their communes are compulsory and that members must hand over all their possessions to the movement.

● The Bible teaches that stealing is wrong. The Children of God will often 'provision' food from supermarkets.

● Followers of the movement are notorious for blasphemy and swearing.

● Members are seldom allowed to communicate with their parents and then only to ask for money. Records are kept on all parents, particularly on their earnings.

● Some parents have claimed that the movement kidnapped and brainwashed their children. In 1972, 60 parents formed the Parents Committee to Free Our Sons and Daughters from the Children of God, known as FREECOG. Shortly afterwards a Texas group, THANKCOG, was formed 'to reassure parents that these accusations aren't true'.

● The Children of God withdrew from America and Britain, saying that Moses David knew that nuclear war would wipe the countries out. Critics have said that the real reason for the departure was increased media pressure and the movement's failure to keep tax records.

CHRISTIAN SCIENCE

God is spirit–spirit is the opposite of matter–therefore God never created matter.

The Church of Christ, Scientist was founded by Mary Baker Eddy over a century ago, and its belief can be summed up in one sentence: God is spirit—spirit is the opposite of matter—therefore God never created matter.

Most people first meet Christian Science in one of two ways. First, there are Christian Science Reading Rooms in towns throughout the 60 countries where the movement operates. Here the enquirer can read the movement's literature. Second, the movement has its own highly-respected international newspaper, the *Christian Science Monitor*, which prints only good news, and has just one religious item each day.

Mary Baker Eddy

Mary Baker was born in Bow, New Hampshire, in 1821. For many years she suffered from a nervous illness which was not helped by an unsympathetic father nor by her three marriages.

She married her first husband, a building contractor, when she was 22. He died soon after their wedding, leaving her with a son and considerable business assets.

Her second husband was an amorous dentist, Dr Patterson, who soon left her, and she later divorced him. However, he did introduce her to an unorthodox healer, Phineas P. Quimby, who refused to use medicine and claimed that there was only one cure for all supposed diseases—the confidence of the patient in the healer. When he cured Mary she spent the next two years lecturing and trying to 'Christianize' Quimby's theories. In later years, however, she denied having learnt from him. Quimby died of a stomach ulcer in 1866. The same year, Mary Baker founded Christian Science and began treating private patients and lecturing.

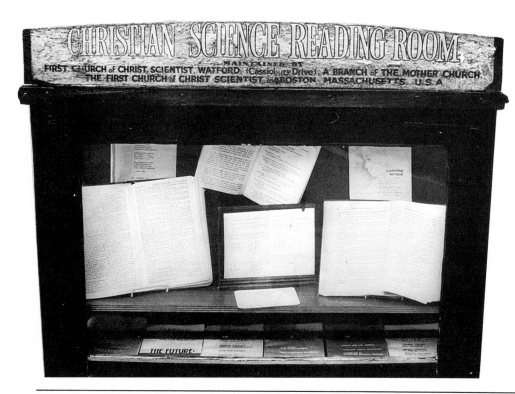

Outside Christian Science churches, literature is always displayed in a reading box. 'I should blush to write this book, as I have, were it of human origin and I apart from God its author; but as I was only a scribe echoing the harmonies of heaven in divine metaphysics, I cannot be supermodest in my estimation of the Christian Science textbook.' Mary Baker Eddy wrote this assessment of her book *Science and Health* in the *Christian Science Journal* in 1901.

The *Illustrated London News* ran a rather uncomplimentary article on the then new faith in December 1906.

Each Sunday, followers in this Christian Science church near London will hear the same message as all other Christian Scientists across the world.

The weekly lesson-sermons are prepared in Boston and sent to all the churches to ensure that everyone is given good basic teaching. There are no preachers; two Readers read the message consisting of a 'Golden Text' and a short passage from the King James/ Authorized Version of the Bible. While parents are at the main service, all those under 20 will be at Sunday School. The church is run by lay people, and each member is expected to be actively involved.

Her third husband, an agent for a sewing-machine manufacturer, was Asa Gilbert Eddy, whom she married when she was 56. He was the first student to announce publicly that he had become a Christian Scientist. Two years earlier Mary had published her world-famous handbook *Science and Health, with Key to the Scriptures* and Eddy now ensured that the movement was put on a firm business footing. When he died in 1882, Mary Baker Eddy said he had been 'mentally assassinated' by one of her more rebellious students.

But her organization continued to grow. She founded a college and a newspaper and continued her lecturing until she died of pneumonia in 1910, aged 89.

Membership rose to more than 300,000 in the 1930s, but since then it has dropped by a third. In America alone, 257 branch churches and 97 Reading Rooms have closed in the last 10 years.

KEY BELIEFS

The teaching of Christian Science is not easy to understand. It is highly philosophical, and double meanings are given to the ordinary words of the Bible.

But it is clear that Christian Science disagrees with almost every fundamental truth of Christianity. Mary Baker Eddy wrote: 'If there had never existed such a Galilean prophet (Jesus) it would make no difference to me' (*Science and Health*, page 318).

God Like Christians, Christian Scientists believe that God is good, that he is spirit and that he desires the best for his people. But they deny his personal character. 'Life, truth and love constitute the triune person called God' (*Science and Health*, page 331).

Jesus Christian Scientists differentiate between the names 'Jesus' and 'Christ'. Page 437 of *Science and Health* is headed 'Jesus is not God'; 'Jesus is the name of the man, who more than all other men, has presented Christ, the divine idea of God.'

The second coming of Jesus 'The second appearing of Jesus is unquestionably the spiritual advent of the advancing idea of God, as in Christian Science' (*Retrospection and Introspection* by Mary Baker Eddy, page 70).

The Holy Spirit Christian Scientists believe that Jesus' promise to his disciples that he would send 'a helper' (the Holy Spirit) refers to Christian Science.

Sin, death, pain and evil All of these are unreal products of our imagination. 'Man is incapable of sin, sickness and death' (*Science and Health*, page 475). 'The body cannot die because matter has no life to surrender.' However, Christian Scientists' views on healing are not consistent. They will go to the dentist or the optician, or to the doctor for a broken leg. Mrs Eddy herself used drugs on many occasions during the last 10 years of her life.

Salvation Jesus' death did nothing to save men from the consequences of their sin.

THE DIVINE LIGHT MISSION

'Maharaj Ji is here. Recognize him, obey him and adore him.'

Guru Maharaj Ji is certainly different from most gurus. He chews gum, loves ice cream and enjoys sports cars and cabin cruisers. Unlike some gurus he encourages his followers to keep their jobs, enjoy good food and make more money, though many have left their jobs to live with other devotees in 'ashrams'.

Thirteen years after his father began the Divine Light Mission in 1960, membership had soared to more than six million. Over the next few years there was a dramatic drop in numbers, but interest is rising again. Followers believe that the Guru Maharaj Ji—or 'Goom Rodgie' as they call him—is the Perfect Master for the present age, who gives 'divine light' or 'knowledge' to his followers so that they can have perfect guidance.

Activities of the religion include a 'divine airline', a publishing company which prints their newspaper *Divine Times* and their magazine *And it is Divine*, second-hand shops called Divine Sales, a New York vegetarian restaurant, a record and film company, an electronics firm, car repairs, laundry services and a food co-op.

Life of a Guru

In 1966 an eight-year-old Indian boy told the weeping mourners at his father's funeral: 'Maharaj Ji is here. Recognize him, obey him and adore him.' Immediately the boy, Shri Sant Ji, was enthroned as the new Perfect Master and took the title Guru Maharaj Ji. The mourners should not have been over-surprised at this: the boy had given his first holy discourse (or 'satsang') when he was two.

The Guru's father, Yogi Raj Paramhans Satguruder Shri Hans Ji Maharaj, founded the Divine Light Mission in 1960 and gave his son 'Knowledge' when he was six. He had begun spreading the basic ideas of the Divine Light Mission in the 1920s after he claimed to have received enlightenment through meditating on knowledge given to him by another guru, Shri Sarupanand Ji. Despite fierce opposition from orthodox Hindu sects, his movement continued to grow and when he died he had millions of disciples.

Today Guru Maharaj Ji and his three older brothers, Bal Bhagwan Ji, Shri Raja Ji and Shri Bhole Ji are all involved in the Divine Light Mission or its rival groups.

The **15-year-old Perfect Master** welcomed 20,000 people to the Alexandra Palace in London in 1971.

KEY BELIEFS

● God is impersonal. He is energy. People are part of that energy.

● God is revealed through incarnations, the 'Perfect Master' for this age being Guru Maharaj Ji.

● Jesus, Buddha, Krishna and Mohammed were all Perfect Masters for their ages.

● 'Christ' is the title applied to every Perfect Master.

● Salvation comes through 'Knowledge' or enlightenment given by the Guru. This Knowledge comes not just from the mind, but from an experience of 'cosmic energy'.

● The Bible is accepted as authentic Scripture, but followers of the Divine Light Mission apply the prophecies of Jesus Christ's Second Coming to Guru Maharaj Ji. Jesus' 'coming in clouds' is said to have been fulfilled when the Guru flew into London Airport. They also believe that Christians have altered the meaning of the Bible.

● To meet 'God' one must go within oneself. Every human has a 'third eye'—the divine eye—which most people are ignorant of. This divine eye is opened by the Perfect Master who makes his followers aware of it by 'taking knowledge' or 'experiencing the light'.

● Ideas and words are unimportant—it is experience which counts.

The controversial guru

The Guru has hit the headlines with many of his exploits.

In November 1972 he was stopped by Indian customs officials in his chartered jumbo jet with a suitcase containing money, watches and jewels valued at £27,000.

Some members who have left the movement claim that they were being brainwashed. After meditating some said they lost the ability to read or do simple arithmetic. According to some former members the main leaders in the movement do little meditation: they need to retain their faculties for administration.

In 1974 the Guru married a former airline stewardess, Marolyn Johnson. This upset his family, especially when he declared that his non-Hindu wife was an incarnation of a ten-armed, tiger-riding Hindu goddess.

In April 1975 the Lord of the Universe was removed as head of the movement by his mother, Shri Mataji, for 'indulging and encouraging his devotees to eat meat, get married, have sexual relations and drink'. She installed his eldest brother Bal Bhagwan Ji as leader of a rival group. Many disciples left and the membership is reported still to be falling today. Meanwhile Guru Maharaj Ji lives quietly with his wife and two children in a mansion overlooking the Pacific in Malibu, California, and has only recently begun active campaigning again.

The Guru in India

About one and a half million people paid homage to the young Perfect Master when he first took his Knowledge to the world in 1970 by driving through Delhi in a golden chariot followed by a procession of camels, elephants and supporters. The Guru, who had left school to start his mission, dropped what his followers called a 'Peace Bomb' when he told the crowd at the India Gate in New Delhi: 'I declare that I will establish peace in this world.'

The Guru in America

Billed as 'the most significant event in the history of mankind', the Divine Light Mission in America sponsored a giant festival in November 1973 entitled *Millennium 73*. It was designed to herald the beginning of the Millennium described in Revelation chapter 20, when Guru Maharaj Ji

would promise an end to human suffering and bring in 1,000 years of peace.

Entrance to the event at Houston Astrodome· was free and up to 200,000 people were expected. As the comet Kohoutek was on its way, some supporters even said visitors from outer space would be coming.

But the event turned out to be a financial flop with less then 20,000 people turning up—and not one from outer space.

The Guru in England

Pop fans at a festival at Glastonbury, England, were amazed when their concert was invaded by a white Rolls Royce. It was driven by the Perfect Master, making his first public appearance in England. He preached for five minutes to the bemused fans—before someone switched off the microphone.

In 1972, some 700 devotees of the Divine Light Mission followed the guru to India. At the Delhi spiritual festival they stayed in tent communities.

GROWING IN DIVINE LIGHT

After receiving Knowledge there are four ways in which a premie can grow spiritually.

Meditation There are four types of meditation which premies are advised to practise for at least two hours a day—seeing divine light, hearing divine music (both inside one's head), tasting divine nectar and perceiving the world within oneself.

Darshan The second way is to see the Guru Maharaj Ji in person, to prostrate oneself before him and touch his feet, showing complete surrender.

Satsang The third way is spiritual discourse.

Service The fourth way is through any physical or mental activity dedicated to the Guru.

Every morning and evening before meditation, premies sing a devotional song to the Guru. Behind the ashram's altar hangs a picture of him. On the altar is usually a cup containing holy water touched by the Guru's feet, which premies drink.

GUIDE TO THE LANGUAGE OF DIVINE LIGHT

Satguru A Hindu word meaning 'one who leads from darkness to light'. It refers to the Perfect Master.

Knowledge The ultimate spiritual experience, given by the Perfect Master.

Mahatma A special disciple who passes on Knowledge from the Perfect Master to other followers.

Premie A devotee of the Guru who has become a member of the Divine Light Mission. The word is Hindi for 'lover'.

Ashram Literally a 'shelter' where premies live. Premies are expected to hand over all their possessions to the Mission; to spend their whole time serving the Mission; to obey the leader of the ashram; to sleep only five hours a day and to abstain from alcohol, drugs, tobacco, meat and sex and any food not provided by the ashram.

Premie house A community house with a less strict routine than an ashram's.

ECKANKAR

Eckankar claims to be 'the highest of all movements', the most ancient of all religious revelations to man.'

Eckankar, which teaches that by 'soul travel' man can enter the Kingdom of Heaven, was 'revived' in 1964 by an American, Paul Twitchell. He claimed to be the 971st Living Eck Master.

Since then the movement has grown rapidly and there are now more than 50,000 'chelas', or students, worldwide.

Paul Twitchell

Twitchell, believed to have been born in Paducah, Kentucky, in 1908 (though he himself gave several birthdates) had always been interested in spiritual matters.

According to him, his grandmother sent him and his sister Kay-Dee to Paris where they met an Indian guru, Sudar Singh. This has been denied by a member of his own family. In 1950 in Washington DC, he and his first wife, Camille, joined an eastern mystic group, Swami Premananda's Self-Revelation Church of Absolute Monism.

But in 1955 disaster struck—his first wife left him and he was asked to leave the church because of misconduct.

That same year, a Hindu mystic, Kirpal Singh toured the United States. He had formed his own movement, 'Ruhani Satsang'—the 'Divine Science of the Soul'—and Twitchell was initiated into the movement though still continuing to dabble in other eastern and occult systems.

Twitchell then wrote *The Tiger's Fang*, telling of his travels with Kirpal Singh through the soul planes. But his leader did not approve, and warned him not to publish. A split developed between the two mystics. Twitchell deleted all references to Singh in *The Tiger's Fang* and said that his revelations had come from a mythical 500-year-old Tibetan monk, Rebazar Tarzs. In 1971 he denied that he even knew of Kirpal Singh.

Eventually in 1964 Twitchell founded a new religion, Eckankar, a 'revived version' of 'a timeless and universal truth'. He wrote articles and gave public lectures on his philosophy and within three years his following had grown from three to several thousands.

He died from a heart attack in a hotel room in Cincinnati, Ohio, on 17 September 1971, but the movement is still continuing under his successor, Darwin Gross.

Eckankar provides 'the way to total awareness ... through the ancient science of soul travel ... the projection of the inner consciousness ... into the ecstatic states.' It is not the only group to promote astral projection—but the reality of the experience is questionable.

It was on the 'astral plane', on 22 October 1971, that Darwin Gross received the Rod of Power from the dead Paul Twitchell, and became the 972nd Living Eck Master.

INCONSISTENCIES IN ECKANKAR

The *Spiritual Counterfeits Project* in the United States listed the following discrepancies in the teaching of Eckankar.

'We do not and cannot know God' (Twitchell, *The Tiger's Fang*).

'It is then we know God' (Twitchell, *Secret Way*).

'No one has realized God except by the path of ECK, for it cannot be done any other way' (Twitchell, *Sharyiat* and *The Precepts of Eckankar*).

'I am aware there are many approaches to the Sugmad (God), for nobody has a monopoly on any path' (Twitchell, *Soul Travel: The Illuminated Way*).

'Jesus . . . was initiated by the (first century) ECK master, Fubbi Quantz' (Twitchell, *Letters to a Chela*).

'Fubbi Quantz, the Living ECK Master during the 10th century in Persia' (Katherine Roe, *Our Ancient Heritage*).

'Jesus' message to the world was a simplified version of Eckankar, which was mangled by his followers and Paul, the founder of Christianity' (Twitchell, *Letters to a Chela*).

'Saint Paul . . . was a member of the secret order of the ECK masters' (Twitchell, *Precepts*).

'It is true one is not paid for any work in ECK except in heavenly dollars' (Darwin Gross, 'Security with ECK' in *ECK World News*, October 1978).

As of June 1977, Darwin Gross drew a declared salary of $2,200 per month (earthly dollars) (Financial declaration of divorce petition).

KEY BELIEFS

● God is everything and everywhere. Eckankar's name for God is 'Sugmad', the everlasting ECK, the 'cosmic current'.

● It is not possible to enter the Kingdom of God except through the teachings of Eckankar.

● The Kingdom of Heaven is composed of eleven different realms. The upper six are 'heavenly'. The lower five are ruled by the devil, 'Kal Niranjan', who causes all the daily problems of the first realm, earth.

● The only way to travel through the realms to reach Sugmad is by 'soul travel'. This is achieved by submitting to the living ECK master, the 'Mahanta'.

● Man has five bodies: the physical body; the astral or emotional body; the causal body, where the recollection of the soul's past experience is kept; the mental body, including the unconscious; the soul body.

● When a person does wrong he must pay back his debt or 'karma'. This payment is made through reincarnation. The soul enters the universe as a mineral and works its way up via plant, fish, reptile and mammal incarnations to the human body. After millions of years it can reach enlightenment. If it abuses the system it will be sent back to the beginning again.

● There is a short cut to God-realization. The presence of the Living Master will burn away the debt of karma.

● There are ten initiations, one for advancing to each realm. These initiations are considered the basic 'sacrament' of Eckankar.

● There are five major forms of soul travel: imaginative projection; meditation; projection via the dream state; trances; direct projection.

GURDJIEFF

Man is spiritually asleep and can rediscover his waking state only by work, discussion, music, dancing and the discovery of his essential unchanging 'I'.

If you haven't heard of Gurdjieff it is hardly surprising. His followers are very shy of publicity. They believe that their message may be lost by being over-simplified. Hence it is difficult to become a follower because it is difficult to find out Gurdjieff's teaching.

The key to this teaching is work. One of Gurdjieff's followers, the author Colin Wilson, wrote: 'From birth until the age of 21 we grow physically and in every other sense. Changes take place inside us without our volition. Then it stops . . . and most people ossify. If growth is to continue unusual efforts must be made in order to stimulate the robot into producing "newness". This was the core of Gurdjieff's work. Its first aim was to defeat man's natural laziness, his tendency to relax and switch off.'

Although Gurdjieff died in 1949 he still has more than 5,000 followers; with many study groups in American cities and university campuses.

A spiritual traveller

George Ivanovich Gurdjieff, known to his followers as 'G', is believed to have been born near the Armenian town of Alexandropol near the Russian–Iranian border in the 1870s. As a young man he was interested in all aspects of the supernatural and even considered becoming a priest. But he became disillusioned with Christianity.

Then he travelled widely for many years, visiting many countries including Tibet. He joined an expedition to find a hidden city in the Gobi Desert and also tried to find an ancient brotherhood which he believed was established in Babylon in 2,500 BC. As well as a traveller he was a keen businessman and became involved in many projects including oilwells, fisheries, carpets and antiques.

After studying a variety of spiritual and occult schools, he believed the time was right to pass on his teaching to the rest of the world. So he arrived in Moscow just before the First World War with a million roubles and began lecturing to the intellectual classes. He gained a sizeable following and came into contact with the Russian mathematician and mystical philosopher Peter Demianovich Ouspensky who had just returned from studying religions in Egypt and India.

Ouspensky did much to spread Gurdjieff's teachings.

But the Russian Revolution came and they both left, Ouspensky going to Britain and Gurdjieff via Istanbul to France. They never saw each other again, largely because of disagreements over teaching. Ouspensky's work was methodical, organized and systematic—the product of a mathematician aiming to make clear his teaching to a wide audience. Gurdjieff's work was always fragmentary, secretive, unpredictable and anti-systematic. He published only two books, *All and Everything* and the autobiographical *Meetings with Remarkable Men*. His followers have maintained the esoteric secrecy of their founder, but the second book has now been made into a major film.

The writer Katherine Mansfield was one of Gurdjieff's followers and went to Fontainebleau in 1932 suffering from tuberculosis. Gurdjieff, who liked to dabble in medicine, told her to ignore her disease and sleep in the loft above the cowshed. Everyone was amazed at her cure—but a week later she died, aged 35.

THE GOLDEN LADDER

Gurdjieff taught that man is ruled by three centres—emotional, intellectual and physical—and most people suffer an imbalance. His aim, the 'fourth way', was to help people to achieve this balance. A person's attitude to life, rather than the lifestyle itself, must change.

Man exists on one of seven rungs of an evolutionary ladder. The ladder can be ascended not by logical knowledge, but by psychological wisdom—self-study, self-awareness, self-remembering and the discovery of the essential unchanging 'I'.

One: instinctive motor man Most people are in this category and enjoy being tossed about through life at the whim of their animal desires and instincts.

Two: emotional man Emotional man is aware of these animal desires and can at least manipulate them.

Three: intellectual man Gurdjieff particularly despised this category of those who think they know everything.

Four: transitional man He is conscious that he wants to change.

Five: integrated man For the first time man acquires some real identity.

Six: conscious man Conscious man begins to acquire super powers of a mental and physical kind.

Seven: the complete man In the final stage, man has acquired everything and is immortal.

Drawing on many mystical ideas, Gurdjieff developed his theories about man and the world. His theory of 'Reciprocal Maintenance' suggests that man both depends on and is responsible for the rest of the world. His role in the world is to improve and increase the 'psychic energy' he can release.

Gurdjieff's base for the last years of his life was the Institute for the Harmonious Development of Man at Fontainbleau, France. Here his followers were given certain tasks to test their critical faculties: work such as washing dishes, scrubbing floors and chopping wood and exercises so complicated that followers sometimes collapsed from exhaustion. Gurdjieff was also notorious for psychic and emotional brutality. He would sometimes pick on a disciple and give him a menial task such as learning by heart a long list of Tibetan words.

Though conditions were hard and food inadequate, once a week there was a feast for all. Drink flowed freely, and he gave a long series of toasts to various 'idiots'. At other times a convoy of cars filled with champagne, caviar and melons would drive into the country for a picnic. Gurdjieff would occasionally take the wheel, but he was a terrible driver and had many crashes, one of which hastened his death in 1949.

THE JEHOVAH'S WITNESSES

They have claimed to be the fastest growing religion in the world. They are well known for visiting homes, usually asking people to have a copy of their magazine.

'They' are the JWs, the Jehovah's Witnesses, the name taken from Isaiah 43:10: 'You are my witnesses, says Jehovah.' And their magazine, *The Watchtower*, has found its way into huge numbers of homes.

Because of their beliefs, Jehovah's Witnesses will not celebrate birthdays, Christmas or Easter; they will not take part in religious education at school; they will not accept blood transfusions, even in the most severe need; they refuse to do military service, to vote or to give allegiance to any country or flag.

Throughout their history this has led to persecution, particularly in Hitler's prison camps. And they are still suffering today behind the Iron Curtain and in some African countries.

Despite efforts to stamp them out, they claim to have more than 3,500,000 members with 65,000 in Britain, 300,000 in America, 77,000 in West Germany and 40,000 in Canada.

The four leaders

'Pastor' Charles Taze Russell, born in 1852 in Pennsylvania, founded the movement. As a teenager he rebelled against his strict Calvinist background and dabbled in oriental studies. He was about to give up religion when an evangelist, Jonas Wendell, convinced him that the Bible was the word of God.

Russell gathered a group of friends together to study the Bible regularly and published their interpretations in a magazine, *Food for Thinking Christians*, later replaced by the bi-monthly *Watchtower*.

He rejected the idea of heaven and hell, but no church would agree with his views. So in 1874 he sold the haberdashery shops he had inherited from his father and founded a new religious organization, the Zion's Watch Tower, in 1879 and incorporated a Zion's Watch Tower Tract Society five years later.

Russell wrote many tracts and a seven-volume series, *Studies in the Scriptures*—the main doctrine of the movement. In it he predicted the end of the world in 1914. However, the date passed and he died in October 1916.

'Judge' Joseph Franklin Rutherford of Missouri, the society's legal counsellor, succeeded Russell. In 1917 he and six other leaders were each jailed for 20 years for their anti-war talk, but he was released nine months later when public hysteria died down at the end of the war.

Until he died in 1942, aged 72, Rutherford successfully ruled the movement with an iron hand. Under his leadership the movement spread worldwide and in 1931 he named his followers 'Jehovah's Witnesses'.

'President' Nathan H. Knorr became the third leader when he was 36. Under his leadership, numbers increased more quickly than at any time in the movement's history. He emphasized education, and several schools, a short-term Bible college at South Lansing, New York, and a radio station have all opened since he took over.

The present leader is Frederick W. Franz, who has had to cope with seriously falling membership. In the past 10 years over a quarter of a million members have left the movement.

Jehovah's Witnesses are the most missionary-minded of religious groups. Every member is regarded as a minister and no one is admitted to membership until he is doing house visiting.

Ordinary members are expected to do 10 hours visiting a month and dispose of at least 12 magazines. 'Pioneers' spend at least 100 hours a month visiting and support themselves with a part-time job. 'Special pioneers' are full-time workers supported by a small allowance.

Even after their plight in Hitler's concentration camps in the Second World War, Jehovah's Witnesses have continued to be persecuted. In a court-martial in Athens in 1966, Christos Kazamis was sentenced to death for refusing to take up arms whilst on military service, because of his beliefs. But at a later trial, shown here, his sentence was changed to four-and-a-half years in prison.

KEY BELIEFS

● They alone proclaim God's truth and the only hope for the world is for everyone to join their movement.

● God is one person, Jehovah, who once existed all alone in space.

● God created Jesus, who in heaven was the archangel Michael. On earth he was a man and not divine. When God raised him from the dead he returned to heaven as a spirit.

● Jesus' death on the cross—or 'torture stake' as they prefer to call it—does not guarantee anyone eternal life. Man can accept this as a ransom for his past sins, but the only guarantee of salvation is continual striving to obey God, as revealed by the Watchtower organization.

● The Holy Spirit is the 'invisible active force that moves his servants to do his will', and is neither personal nor God.

● All other churches, and all governments, are controlled by the devil.

● The present world system will end soon with the Battle of Armageddon. Those who survive will reign with Christ for 1,000 years.

● During this time there will be neither disease nor death nor any unhappiness. Flowers and fruit will grow abundantly and wild animals will become tame.

● After 1,000 years all the dead will be raised up. Those 144,000 who reach the required standard will live in heaven; the vast majority will live on earth. Those who reject their teachings will be annihilated.

● God's kingdom on earth was established in 1914, when Christ returned to his temple and began to cleanse it. The devil was cast out of heaven and God fully established this part of his kingdom. The earthly part of his kingdom will be set up within the lifetime of those alive in 1914. Every earthquake, famine, war and catastrophe is a sign of the end which is coming soon. 'Many now living will not see death' is one of the JW's favourite themes.

Their church

Once a year Jehovah's Witnesses observe 'Memorial' (Holy Communion) claiming it should be held on the biblical anniversary of Christ's death, the 14th day of the Jewish month of Nisan. Memorial and baptism are the only formal parts of worship. The rest consists of ministry school for Bible analysis, service meetings for training in visiting, public lectures and regular Sunday study of the current issue of the *Watchtower*.

Their movement is as efficient as a commercial company. The 'Board of Directors' is the all-powerful group at the head. Under them are 'Religious Servants' and beneath them are 'Zone Servants' who are responsible for the local groups known as 'Companies' which meet in the Kingdom Hall. The 'Service Director' is at the head of each company and is responsible to the

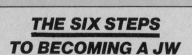

THE SIX STEPS TO BECOMING A JW

Initial visit During the first visit the Jehovah's Witness aims to introduce himself and leave some literature. Many who think the best way to get rid of him is to take some literature find that this is the surest way to guarantee another visit.

Back-call Every potential convert will receive a second visit when the JWs will try to find out his reaction to the literature. They will also try to arrange a Home Study Group.

Home Study Group The contact will be encouraged to bring friends to study some of the publications

in his home. After a few weeks he will join a larger group to look at the teachings in more detail.

The Kingdom Hall After home study, the contact will be invited to the Kingdom Hall. Here he will receive VIP treatment and as he has been prepared in advance he will understand the teaching.

Visiting He will then be expected to attend mid-week lectures and learn how to go door-to-door visiting.

Baptism The final stage in becoming a Jehovah's Witness is to be baptized.

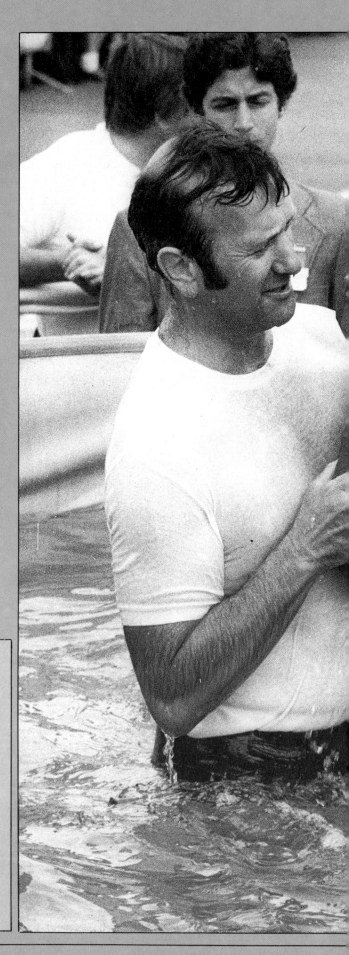

Zone Servant for running his company. He is assisted by a 'Service Committee' which is particularly concerned with visiting.

Falling numbers

Witnesses are highly dedicated to a movement which, to outsiders, appears to be joyless and suppressive. But their zeal in spreading their message has been tempered since 1975. Witnesses had been led to believe that the final Battle of Armageddon would happen in October 1975. Membership mushroomed and many followers left their jobs and sold their homes. But since the time came and went without incident, they have had to come to terms with the fact that they had been misled and many members have left after years in the movement.

Baptism is the final step of commitment in becoming a Jehovah's Witness. At mass rallies, many hundreds of followers are baptized at the same time. In 1978, the movement took over the Twickenham rugby ground in London, and this mass baptism took place in a specially-built pool.

ARE THEY GOD'S WITNESSES?

● They quote the Bible, but their *New World Translation* is inaccurate. (For example, they translate the first verse of John's Gospel: 'Originally the Word was, and the Word was with God, and the Word was *a* god.' The 'a' before the final word is not in the original Greek. Its inclusion relegates Jesus to a secondary god.)

● Verses are taken out of context to back up their beliefs. Witnesses forbid blood transfusions and will let a member die if necessary, often quoting Leviticus 3:17, 7:26–27 and 17:10–14. But these passages are nothing to do with blood transfusions.

● Members believe that Jesus has already returned invisibly to the world. This conflicts with Revelation 1:7 which says of Jesus' second coming: 'Every eye will see him.'

● Russell said he was a competent Greek scholar and claimed that all existing Bible translations were unreliable. However, it was proved in court in Canada that he could not read Greek, though he had sworn under oath that he could.

● Another controversy was Russell's 'Miracle Wheat' sold for one dollar a pound, which was claimed to outgrow other seeds by as much as five times. He tried to sue a paper for $100,000 for labelling the claims a fake, but lost his case when government examiners could find no distinct superiority in the grain.

● In 1947 the Supreme Court of Canada ruled that Jehovah's Witnesses 'were not a religious body'.

KRISHNA CONSCIOUSNESS

'Hare Krishna, Hare Krishna, Krishna, Krishna, Hare Hare, Hare Rama, Hare Rama, Rama, Rama,' they chanted.

His Divine Grace A. C. Bhakdivedanta Swami Prabhupada at a press conference on his arrival in Britain. His teaching first took root in America, but has now spread throughout the world.

With their saffron robes, heads completely shaven except for an isolated pigtail, cloth bags round their necks containing their prayer beads and ash marks on their faces, the young men on the street corners danced and swayed to the drumbeat.

The public display over the past few years by members of the International Society for Krishna Consciousness (ISKCON) had two purposes. First, they believed that by chanting their god's name ('Hare' means Lord and Krishna is the name of their god) they could liberate their souls from the evil influence of their bodies. Second, as they chanted they publicized their teachings by selling their magazine *Back to Godhead* and raising money for the movement.

Today their publicity is less eye-catching. More often dressed in jeans and jerseys, they offer records and literature free to passers-by . . . but a donation is asked for.

They have more than 70 centres throughout the world with about 15,000 followers. There are about 10,000 in America, less than 1,000 in Britain and only four or five centres in India, the home of the movement.

One of the most famous supporters is the ex-Beatle George Harrison who has given the movement its headquarters near London and whose song about Hare Krishna, 'My Sweet Lord', reached number one in the charts.

Apart from donations the main source of income is a large factory in Los Angeles run by Hare Krishna followers who make and sell incense.

Many of the followers are former drug addicts and the group's success in getting them to kick the habit has led to praise from the mayors of New York and San Francisco.

KEY BELIEFS

● Krishna is the highest of the Hindu gods, the Lord, the Absolute Truth. He has had many incarnations.

● Jesus was not God. He was a pure devotee of Krishna, visiting from another planet.

● The Hindu Scriptures are authoritative. The Bible and the Koran are genuine Scriptures but have become distorted in translation and interpretation over the centuries.

● After death the soul is reincarnated. The way one lives this life will determine the form one will have in the next life.

● Salvation lies in purification, in complete surrender and devotion to Krishna.

● Men are superior to women.

● Any action done for Krishna cannot be bad. Krishna is above both good and evil.

KRISHNA CONSCIOUSNESS

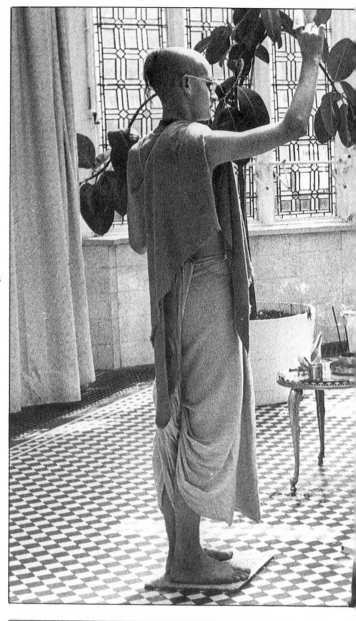

At the movement's headquarters, Bhaktivedanta Manor, Letchmore Heath, followers attend to the statues of Hindu gods each day. Followers take on a new Indian name and a whole new way of life.

The Founder

His Divine Grace A.C. Bhaktivedanta Swami Prabhupada started his mission to the West in 1965 when he was 70. Wearing a yellow gown he sat under a tree in New York's Greenwich village chanting a mantra.

More than 30 years earlier he had been told by his guru in India to spread the message to America.

Prabhupada, born in Calcutta in 1896, did not leave India until 11 years after he retired from his job as manager of a chemical factory in 1954. He won a patron, and Sumati Moraji, the owner of India's largest shipping company, gave him a berth on a ship to America and some money to get him started.

At first he slept in a Yoga centre and he set up his own headquarters only when a follower gave him a month's rent.

He began giving classes and many joined him, particularly hippies and young intellectuals disillusioned with materialism. They became his missionaries who took his message all over the world.

In 1977 the founder died leaving the leadership in the hands of an international 12-member Governing Board Commission.

Life in the movement

Followers of Hare Krishna live in temples and must submit themselves completely to their leader, the Temple President. He in turn must ultimately answer to the governing body of 12 and carry out their orders. He must offer spiritual guidance, see that sufficient funds are obtained, ensure rules are kept, be the final authority on scriptural and ceremonial procedures and arrange members' marriages.

Around the temple are statues of deities considered to be incarnations of Krishna in material forms. These have to be dusted, dressed and fed every morning. Followers bathe the statues in a liquid of rose water, milk and a small amount of cow's urine. After the ceremony it is considered an honour to drink the liquid.

Children of Hare Krishna followers go to special schools where learning how to advance in spiritual life is as much a part of the curriculum as reading, writing and arithmetic.

BECOMING A FOLLOWER

Pre-initiation stage A person who wishes to join the movement must prove himself. He usually takes part in temple life for six months and is taught the movement's philosophy.

Initiation When a person is considered suitable for membership the temple president presides over 'harer name', an elaborate fire ceremony when a member is given a new spiritual Sanskrit name and three strands of neck beads which he must wear until he dies.

Brahmin Six months later those who are faithful members and have advanced spiritually are eligible for a second rite, the brahminical initiation. Here the follower is given a secret mantra which is to be chanted three times a day. Men also receive a sacred thread which is worn over the shoulder and across the chest.

Sannyasa Only a few members achieve the final stage, reserved for especially devoted men. They must make a life-long vow of poverty, celibacy and commitment to preach and do good works.

LIFESTYLE

Cleanliness Washing is an important feature of the movement. A follower will take many showers every day, especially every time he returns to the temple.

Sex Outside marriage, sexual relations are strictly forbidden. Intercourse is permitted between married couples only once a month for the purpose of procreation, not pleasure. Before sex the couple must chant 50 rounds on their prayer beads to purify themselves.

Food Alcohol, tobacco, tea, coffee, eggs, meat and fish are all banned. Eating is seen as an act of worship and all food is offered to Krishna and so is spiritual (prasadam).

Medicine Medicines are taken only when absolutely necessary.

Games No frivolous sports, games or gambling are allowed. Time is important. Any time not given to deepening their own devotion to Krishna should be given to spreading the devotion to others.

3 a.m.	Get up and have a shower
3–4	Personal chanting using prayer beads, or 'japa'
4–4.30	Service, with men on one side of the room and women and children on the other.
4.30–6	Individual chanting
6–7	Study hour reading the *Bhagavad Gita*, their sacred Scripture. A verse is chanted in Sanskrit, then it is explained and members ask questions
7.30	Breakfast
8–10	Clean up and do chores in the temple
10–6	On the streets raising money, with a short lunch break back at the temple
6	Meal
6.30–7	Study
7	Service
8.15	Hot milk
8.30–10	Study once any chores have been done
10–3	Sleep

MEHER BABA

'There is no doubt of my being God personified... I am the Christ... I am everything and I am beyond everything.'

The self-proclaimed Messiah from India who never said a word for 43 years attracted much interest from the media and many young people in the 1960s.

Many students and hippies became followers of Meher Baba and set up chapters of Meher Baba Centres in universities and colleges throughout America. Commitment to him is very emotional. Some followers keep photographs of him in their lockets or have posters of him above their beds.

It was back in 1921 that he gathered his first disciples (called 'manadali') and established an 'ashram' or community near Bombay. Here his disciples called him Meher Baba, which means 'compassionate father'.

After training his followers he organized a colony at Meherabad, near Ahmednagar, 70 miles north-east of Poona, India. This is still the centre for the worldwide movement which now has more than 7,000 members, its own quarterly magazine *The Awakener* and a publishing house.

The making of a saviour

Meher Baba was born Merwan Sheriar Irani, in Poona, India, to Iranian parents. One day in 1913, at the age of 19, he was riding his bicycle when he met an elderly Muslim woman, Hazrat Babajan, who was known as the great mystic of her time.

She kissed him on the forehead and 'tore away the veil which obscured my own God-realization'. He then knew that he was a saviour, the last of the great incarnations of God.

For three days he lay as though he was dead. It took nine months before he returned to normal awareness, during which time he neither ate nor slept.

Eight years later he founded his first community or 'ashram' in Bombay. He opened various hospitals and schools to help the needy. Thousands flocked to him but he suddenly closed the whole operation. His only explanation was, 'Often my external activities and commitments are only the external expressions of the internal work I am doing.'

The years of silence

Just as suddenly, when he was 31, he stopped speaking. He considered that God had laid down enough principles and said enough words—now he had to show how to live them.

From that time on he communicated only by hand signals and an alphabet board. He also wrote many books, including a five-volume work entitled *Discourse*, and *God Speaks*, which outlined the story of God and the universe.

In his *Universal Message*, Meher Baba wrote: 'When I break my silence, the impact of my love will be universal and all life in creation will know, feel and receive of it. It will help every individual to break himself free from his own bondage in his own way. I am the Divine Beloved who loves you more than you can ever love yourself. The breaking of my silence will help you to help yourself in knowing your real Self.'

But on 31 January 1969 at the age of 74, he died—or as his followers said 'dropped his body'—not having said a word for the last 43 years.

KEY BELIEFS

● Meher Baba was the final and greatest incarnation of God. The others were Zoroaster, Krishna, Rama, Buddha, Jesus and Mohammed.

● Followers must lose their identity and surrender completely to Meher Baba.

● Man's soul progresses through reincarnation. The soul begins as a stone and then moves into a metal. It continues its evolutionary journey via vegetables, insects, reptiles, fish, birds and animals. Finally the soul moves from a monkey to a human being. There are then seven planes of human existence and if a person misuses his spiritual powers as he works his way up to the fifth plane of sainthood, then he could be sent all the way back to a stone in his next incarnation. The sixth plane is the plane of illumination and the final one is Nirvana, merger into the mind of God.

'The book that I shall make people read is the book of the heart, which holds the key to the mystery of life.' Meher Baba found the way to the hearts of thousands of followers, best-known of whom is Pete Townshend of The Who.

The Meher Baba Centre

At Myrtle Beach, South Carolina, is the largest of the Meher Baba centres in America. Up to 3,000 people a year visit this shrine which contains Meher Baba's shiny blue Ford Sedan, a large meeting-hall which he used and his fully-furnished six-roomed bungalow where his robe, white underpants and locks of hair are on display. Nearby is a blood-stained pillow where his head rested after a car crash. He was involved in many crashes; according to one follower, this was to fulfil a prophecy that he would shed blood on American soil.

WAS MEHER BABA GOD?

Meher Baba claimed to be an incarnation of God, comparable with Jesus Christ. So how does he compare?

Meher Baba	Jesus Christ
Meher Baba holds out no hope for the sinner—his soul will return to stone.	Jesus offers hope and forgiveness to all.
Meher Baba died of natural causes—his body remains in the ground.	Jesus died claiming that his death provided the forgiveness of sins. He then rose from the dead to prove it.
Meher Baba died without breaking his silence—the great act which he had promised would free mankind.	Jesus completed his work on earth. On the cross he said: 'It is finished.'
Meher Baba's followers must lose their identity in him.	Surrender to Christ involves no loss of identity. On the contrary, in him believers become fully the people they are meant to be.

THE MOONIES

'Would you buy a candle to help youth work?'
'Will you give a donation to missionary work?' Many busy
shoppers when asked such questions willingly pay up.

The 'Perfect Father', Sun Myung Moon. Members of his Unification Church follow him with a deep devotion. They base their whole lives on his teaching, which they learn from his book *The Divine Principle* and from his continuing proclamations. Moon begins these speeches with the phrase 'Master speaks . . .'.

Unknowingly, shoppers raised almost £1 million in Britain alone between March 1978 and March 1979 for the Moonies, the religious group named after their leader, the Reverend Sun Myung Moon. The group has many other names, including the Holy Spirit Association for the Unification of World Christianity.

If a passer-by expresses interest he will be invited to their local centre to find out more. There he will receive the 'loving treatment'—an hour's chat over coffee before one of the leaders talks to him alone about the movement. Then he will probably be invited back for a meal and further discussion.

The argument presented runs like this: 'Everyone is eventually going to belong to the Unification Church, so why not join the Church now. Moreover, those who fight against Mr Moon will suffer'.

Those interested in joining are sent on a course

for a weekend, one, two or three weeks, where they are given intensive teaching. If they wish to join, they are encouraged to give up their job, home and possessions and live at one of the Church's centres.

The Church has been growing rapidly in numbers—many of them young people between 18 and 26—and in wealth. The Moonies claim to have more than 3 million members in more than 140 countries, although others put that figure much lower. They say there are 3,000 followers in Britain but the figure is probably more like 1,000.

Mr Moon's financial empire is said to be worth more than £35 million with a network of 80 businesses ranging from pharmaceutical firms to factories producing spare parts for military weapons.

The Church has also invested in property, including three lavish estates near New York costing more than $2 million.

The Rev Sun Myung Moon

When Sun Myung Moon was sixteen he said that Jesus appeared to him while he was praying on a mountain in North Korea and told him to restore God's perfect Kingdom on earth.

During the next nine years which included a course of study in electrical engineering in Japan, he said the Church's beliefs were revealed to him by God, Jesus, Moses and Buddha. This theology was later written up as a book, *The Divine Principle*, by one of Moon's followers, Yee Hye Wen.

In 1945 as a member of an underground Pentecostal movement he began preaching. But he upset the North Korean government and was sent to a labour camp for three years until UN forces freed him. His followers say that he was imprisoned for his anti-Communist views; his opponents claim that it was for bigamy and adultery.

When he moved to South Korea and founded the Unification Church in 1954 his wife left him. He said: 'My wife could not understand my mission.' Moon married for a second time—though there are claims that he has married at least four times.

He began building a multi-million pound network of industries and as he climbed the financial ladder the government in South Korea

began to look on him more favourably.

Moon believes that Communism is evil and is the main obstacle to the creation of the Kingdom of God on earth. He believes that the UN is a stage for the Communists, and so he has founded a number of anti-Communist groups, including the International Federation For Victory Over Communism.

He claimed that God appeared to him on 1 January 1972 telling him to prepare the world for the second coming of the Messiah.

In America he has been met by demonstrations, with some labelling him fascist because of his support for the South Korean government.

Mr Moon also tried to become involved in US politics. In 1974 he launched a 'God loves Richard M. Nixon campaign' when the Watergate scandal was just breaking. However, he remained quiet when Nixon was found guilty.

KEY BELIEFS

● The Unification Church is not a denomination but a movement to save the world.

● The *Divine Principle*, the movement's book of theology, is the latest revelation from God.

● God wanted Adam and Eve to form a 'trinity' with him and have perfect children to build his Kingdom. His desires were frustrated when Eve was sexually seduced by Satan, thereby starting a new 'trinity'—Adam, Eve and Satan.

● God therefore chose Jesus as the Second Adam, who was to create a holy family. But Jesus, a perfect man though not the Son of God, was rejected by the people and crucified before he could get married.

● God's second best for Jesus was the resurrection, which produced only a spiritual salvation. If Jesus had married and raised a family, he would have laid the foundation for man's full salvation.

● As Jesus accomplished only a partial salvation, a new Messiah is needed.

● The new Messiah, the Lord of the Second Advent, will come into the world and marry a perfect woman. They will form a 'trinity' with God and will have perfect children. Heaven will come upon earth and mankind will be brought back to God.

● The Second Coming of the Messiah will be in secret and has indeed already happened. Korea, the descendant of the ten lost tribes of biblical Israel, is to be the new Israel and the new Messiah was due to be born there around 1920. (Mr Moon was born in Korea in 1920—but he is reluctant to admit publicly that he is the Lord of the Second Advent.)

● The sins of the members of the Church and of their ancestors must be paid for by non-stop exertion. The movement stresses continual activity as the way to prevent temptation by Satan.

● Jews suffer from 'collective sin', because they crucified Christ.

● The faithful will enter the Kingdom of Heaven in families—hence the importance of marriage.

THE MOONIES

ARE THEY OF THE HOLY SPIRIT?

● They claim to be highly moralistic—yet some followers admit they practise 'heavenly deception' to raise money.

● Supporters of Mr Moon—'The Reverend' is a courtesy title—say he is the new Messiah come to save the world. Opponents, including those who have left the church, claim members are brainwashed. Some, pointing to Moon's militant anti-Communist views and support for the former South Korean dictator, Park Chung Hee, say that the movement has been used as a front for South Korean intelligence.

● Mr Moon told Americans that the Messiah would arrive in 1980–81 and that the salvation of the world depended on whether they repented within the decade. A true prophet is one whose prophecies happen, says the Bible.

● The Presbyterian Church in Korea ruled that the Unification Church was heretical because: (1) Sun Myung Moon has placed himself more than Jesus Christ as the object of their faith. (2) Their doctrine violates the morals of modern society. (3) They would destroy the Christian church by deceiving pure and sincere Christians.

LIFESTYLE

Business The movement 'wants to promote new standards in industry and business, giving quality of produce and concern for the customer'. Their network of businesses ranges from factories in Korea making tools, weapon parts and ginseng tea to a Tokyo-based company which markets honey from China.

Morals The church promotes high moral standards and aims 'to return to Christian principles in public life'. Smoking and drugs are banned. In Britain the Church supports the Viewers and Listeners Association in its campaign to clean up broadcasting.

Community life Many members live in communities spending much of their time in prayer, singing and physical exercise. Moonies always carry 'holy salt' with them to sprinkle on their food to purify it. If they spend a night away from the community they will sprinkle the salt around their new surroundings, often opening the doors and windows to let evil spirits leave.

Worship Every Sunday morning the Moonies hold a 'pledge service' at which men wear suits and women dresses. Women sit on the left and men on the right before a table containing a bowl of flowers and a picture of Sun Myung Moon. The group bows three times to the Heavenly Father and the true parents, Mr Moon and his wife. Then everyone repeats a pledge in unison, recommitting themselves to the Unification Church. After a 20-minute prayer from one of the leaders the service finishes with everyone praying aloud together. They believe God will accept their prayer only if it is pure.

Parents' opposition

Many parents, worried that their children have been brainwashed into joining the Unification Church, have formed groups to lobby governments and to get their children out of the movement.

In Britain MP Paul Rose founded *FAIR*—The Family, Action, Information and Rescue—to help relatives, friends and ex-cult members. In America more than 1,000 families contacted the Dutchess District Attorney complaining that the Church had exercised some type of mind control over their children.

Then in February 1976 more than 300 parents and ex-cult members gathered in Washington for a 'Day of Affirmation and Protest' to demand an investigation into the Church and other groups. Senator Robert Dole of Kansas was presented with the 14,000-name petition.

For parents who go to the courts to get their children back, costs become enormous and some have had to mortgage their homes to find the money. Many parents have found other methods. Some have hired people to remove their children forcibly from the Church and to de-programme them to overcome their brainwashing.

The world's biggest wedding service. Sun Myung Moon married 791 couples at a mass ceremony in Seoul, South Korea, in October 1970.

Members of the Unification Church submit a list of five potential marriage partners to their leaders, who then make the final choice.

Sex before marriage is forbidden and even within marriage partners abstain from sex for several years so that their offspring's blood will be 'pure'.

Divorce is allowed only if a partner leaves the Unification Church.

THE MORMONS

'May we come in and discuss the Bible with you?' ask two well-groomed young men on the doorstep. For many people, that is the first introduction to the Mormons.

According to the Church of Jesus Christ of Latter-Day Saints there are 10,000 of their young Mormon missionaries working at any one time to try to add to their 6 million followers throughout the world. They claim to make 180,000 converts a year in the 51 countries where they are working.

Mormon families consider it a privilege to let their sons go abroad for two years of missionary service, paying their own way as they go door-to-door visiting.

The headquarters of the church is Salt Lake City in Utah, a state where 60 per cent of the people are Mormons. Because of Mormonism the state has an excellent reputation for its work in public health, education and social services. And the people are renowned for their honesty, cheerfulness and hard work.

Joseph Smith

But despite the sincerity and real faith and devotion of today's Mormons, the origin of the movement remains very dubious. Joseph Smith

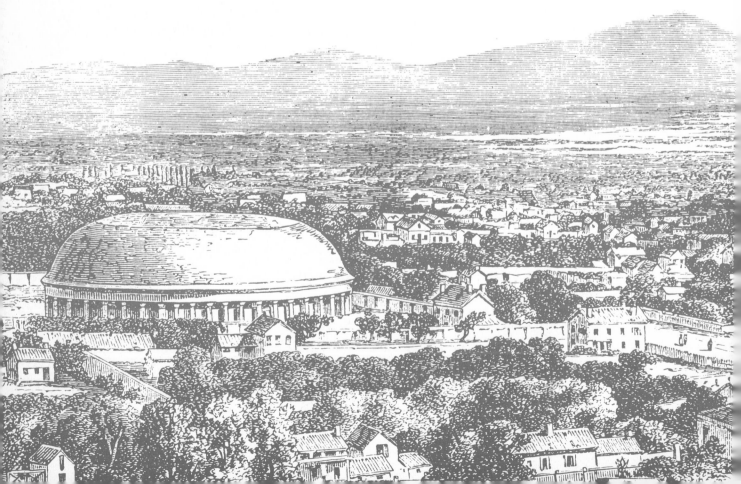

was born in Sharon, Vermont, in 1805. When he was 15 he said God appeared to him and told him not to join any of the churches as 'all their creeds were abomination'.

Three years later an angel, Moroni, told him to go to the Hill of Cumorah, near Palmyra, New York, where he would find a book written with gold plates telling the history of the early Americans and the complete gospel.

Although the writing was said to be in ancient Egyptian hieroglyphs the angel told him he would be able to translate it with the aid of some spectacles to be found nearby. He claims to have found the plates and the spectacles but Moroni told him not to touch them for four years. Joseph Smith, who was illiterate, obeyed.

It was not until 1827 that he began dictating from behind a screen to three scribes what is now known as *The Book of Mormon*. Moroni then took the gold plates and spectacles back from Joseph Smith.

On 6 April 1830 as the book was being published, Smith and five supporters founded the Church of Jesus Christ of Latter-Day Saints at Fayette, New York State. Although he soon had many followers he faced much ridicule and opposition forced him to keep moving around.

When some of his closest friends left and began to expose Smith and his alleged immorality in a newspaper, Smith ordered the printing offices to be destroyed.

He appealed to the state governor but Joseph Smith, his brother and two others were arrested and remanded in custody until his trial. But it never took place—a mob stormed the prison at Nauvoo and murdered Smith in 1844.

Salt Lake City is the 'promised land' of the Mormons. When persecution of the first Mormons came to a head in 1844 with the murder of Joseph Smith, his successor, Brigham Young, led hundreds of Mormons on a flight to the west. When they reached the Great Salt Lake, they began to plough the land and plant crops.

Others followed and together they built a great city and a nation of their own out of the desert.

Their faith and industry were rewarded when Utah was admitted to the union of the United States in 1895.

In the middle of the city is the Genealogical Society, where Mormons can explore their ancestry in order to baptize their dead forbears.

THE MORMONS

KEY BELIEFS

- Only Mormons will go to heaven.

- Joseph Smith is the true Messiah—Jesus was his forerunner.

- *The Book of Mormon* is God's latest revelation. It has equal authority with the Bible.

- God is an exalted man. He has a physical body and is the same person as Adam.

- God had sexual relations with Mary to conceive Jesus.

- Jesus, who did not exist before his birth on earth, was polygamously married to Mary, Martha and Mary Magdalene.

- A person can earn his own salvation by good works.

- The Mormon priesthood is the Kingdom of God. To disobey them is to disobey God.

- Only by total immersion in baptism can sins be forgiven. If a loved one has died, a Mormon can be baptized in his place to get him to heaven.

- A man will retain his wives in heaven and have children there. Although polygamy was introduced by divine revelation to Joseph Smith, it was abandoned after government pressure. Today Mormons have a 'celestial marriage', a wedding service to last for eternity.

- In the past many leaders have said that negroes were inferior to white men and were under God's curse. Black people were not allowed to become priests. But this ruling has been changed recently.

- Before Jesus returns to earth to reign for 1,000 years Mormons will be gathered together and the Jews will return to Jerusalem.

- During Christ's 1,000-year reign on earth, Mormons will build temples to remain on earth and be worthy of a 'second chance'

- During this time everyone will live to the age of 100—then suddenly be made immortal.

- At the end of the 1,000 years there will be a second resurrection and all will be judged. Those worthy of the highest grade of salvation will live on the new earth, the others being put elsewhere. The third of the spirit world who rebelled before creation and a small number of humans guilty of the worst sins will spend eternity in hell.

The Book of Mormon says...

The Book of Mormon teaches many things about the history of America. According to the book, an Israelite, Lehi, and his family and friends escaped from Jerusalem in 586 BC, built a boat and started sailing east round the world. With the aid of a compass they landed in America and from Lehi's family sprang two nations of people who became the ancestors of the American Indians. For 1,000 years they recorded their history on plates in an unknown language. Before they were wiped out in AD 421 the last survivor, Moroni, buried the plates in a hillside.

After his resurrection Jesus visited America and founded a new church because his hopes in the Old World had been dashed. Jesus will return to earth and establish his Kingdom in America.

LIFESTYLE

True Mormons live very carefully according to a high moral code.

- They give a tenth of their income to the church.

- They fast once a month. They will eat meat only in moderation.

- They will not smoke, nor drink alcohol, or coffee or tea, even though the artificial stimulant in these is minimal.

- Families have special study evenings when they will sing, pray, play games and discuss family problems.

- They support 'Youth and recreational programmes' to draw in young people to the faith.

Mission is a key part of Mormons' activity. Many young Mormons spend two years as unpaid missionaries, working long hours in systematic door-to-door visiting.

The world's most famous young Mormon missionaries—the seven members of the pop group, the Osmonds. The seven, Marie, Jimmy, Donny, Jay, Merril, Wayne and Alan are all members of the Mormon Church and were brought up in Utah, USA. Their seven gold records have boosted the Mormon image and led to some of their fans becoming Mormons.

ARE THEY LATTER-DAY SAINTS?

● *The Book of Mormon* covers from 600 BC to AD 400—yet there are many direct parallels with the Authorized/King James Bible, translated in AD 1611.

● A Mormon leader claimed the way *The Book of Mormon* was translated ruled out any possibility of error. 3,000 changes have been made to the book since 1830.

● Mormons claim that the truth of *The Book of Mormon* can be proved by the archaeology of America. W. Duncan Strong of New York's Columbia University said, 'I do not believe there is a single thing of value concerning the pre-history of the American

Indian in *The Book of Mormon* and I believe the great majority of American archaeologists would agree with me.'

● Mormons claim Professor Charles Anthon of Columbia University vouched for the genuineness of the plates. The professor said in a letter to a friend: 'The whole story about my having pronounced the Mormonite inscription to be "reformed hieroglyphs" is perfectly false.'

● In the preface to *The Book of Mormon*, Oliver Cowdery, David Whitmer and Martin Harris claim an angel showed them the plates and engravings. All three

witnesses later said they had seen them with 'the eye of faith' and renounced Mormonism.

● Was *The Book of Mormon* from God or not? Between 1809 and 1812 a Solomon Spaulding wrote an imaginary history of two civilizations coming to America. He died and the manuscript was left in the printer's office. A compositor at the office, Sidney Rigdon, met Joseph Smith and became a Mormon. Later Mrs Spaulding, the widow of Solomon said *The Book of Mormon* was her husband's work—an allegation hotly denied by the Mormons.

● Though Mormonism today is

highly moral, its original leaders were rather less so. In 1834, 62 of his neighbours signed a petition saying Smith and his father were 'entirely destitute of moral character and addicted to vicious habits'. Later Joseph Smith was found guilty of forging bank notes. Brigham Young left 17 wives, 56 children and a fortune of £400,000. He was utterly ruthless with disillusioned members who tried to leave Salt Lake City soon after the long march and some who tried to escape were murdered by him and his supporters.

THE PEOPLE'S TEMPLE

'All my life I have endured the pain of poverty and suffered many disappointments and heartaches common to mankind. For that reason I try to make others happy and secure.'

Jim Jones, leader of the People's Temple Church, regularly ordered his followers to drink an unknown liquid and syringe some into their children's mouths, telling them death would follow in 45 minutes. When the time had passed he told them the 'white night ritual' was to test their loyalty to the cause.

On 18 November 1978, 913 members including Jones and 260 children drank the liquid at their jungle settlement in Jonestown, Guyana, South America. However, this time it was laced with cyanide. The death of all 913 took less than five minutes.

Who was Jim Jones—'Dad' to his followers— and how could he have such control over them?

Jim Jones was once a respected social leader, with carefully developed political alliances. By the end he was a paranoid dictator, surviving on alternate stimulants and tranquillizers.

Jim Jones

James Warren Jones was born on 13 May 1931, in Indiana in the tiny mid-western town of Lynn (main industry, coffin making).

He preached his first sermon to a group of children when he was 12. Two years later his parents separated and he lived with his mother until he married a local nurse when he was 18.

Jones studied at Indiana University but gave up after a year to spend his time preaching. He obtained a degree at night school and became a pastor at a Methodist Church. But he left after a disagreement over doctrine.

He then founded his own church and he came up with what must be the most novel way yet to raise money to buy a church building—he began selling South American spider monkeys door-to-door.

In a shrewd move he affiliated his People's Temple Church with the Disciples of Christ. This allowed him to say he was an officially ordained minister of a 1.4-million-member Christian denomination.

He believed in practical Christianity and opened a soup kitchen for down-and-outs and two nursing homes for the elderly and sick. He also adopted a Korean and two coloured children.

After attending a spiritualist meeting in 1950 he began to believe in reincarnation and to denounce the Bible as an idol.

Still God's heir on earth, as he called himself, he began attracting more and more people to his temple to see 'miracle' healings—all of which were fakes.

In 1964 he prophesied that the world would be engulfed in thermonuclear war on 15 July 1967. Many gave up everything to follow him from Indiana to Northern California where he assured them they would be safe.

Ten years later, his first prophecy forgotten, he said persecution was about to begin and many fled with him to a refuge in the Amazon jungle which the movement had bought for $1 million.

Investigations begin

Those who left the People's Temple claimed the movement allowed bizarre sexual activities, brainwashing of members, and ritualistic beating of children. Informing on other members was encouraged, and there were interrogation

WHY DID IT HAPPEN?

What led to this mass death? Mel White in his book *Deceived* suggests the following factors.

● Jones created a brilliant illusion of respectability, by public relations, flattery, intimidation and favours. He had dined with the First Lady, Mrs Rosalyn Carter, flown with Vice-President Walter Mondale in his private jet and had been appointed the first full-time director of a human rights commission by the Mayor of Indianapolis.

● He undermined the authority of both the Bible and the church. He outlined various 'errors and contradictions' in the Bible which a theologian would see through but which could disturb an ordinary Christian.

● Temple members were kept in a state of exhaustion, psychological isolation and poverty. Defection was difficult in America, almost impossible in Guyana.

● Members feared Jones and were kept in sexual bondage. Break-up of partnerships was encouraged. Jones expected and encouraged sexual preference for himself from both men and women.

sessions and threats of reprisals for defecting. Some who did leave died mysteriously soon afterwards.

Hardly anyone took much notice of these stories except US Congressman Leo Ryan. He was eventually given an invitation to visit the jungle headquarters and on 17 November 1978, he and some journalists, lawyers and relatives set off in a chartered plane.

Smiling and dancing hosts and hostesses looked after their visitors very well during their stay. Everything seemed to be going well until a grandmother begged Ryan to get her out and then 20 others followed her.

One of Jones's aides tried to stab Ryan but he was pulled away and the congressman and his group escaped towards their aircraft.

But before they could get away seven of them were shot dead—three journalists, three defectors and Ryan.

White night

'Alert, alert, alert' screamed the loudspeakers just after 5 p.m. Jones's followers hurriedly gathered round him in a huge semi-circle.

'Dad' told them Ryan's plane would be shot down and that 'they' would come parachuting into the settlement for revenge. His congregation knew 'they' referred to the CIA, fascists or mercenaries.

'If we can't live in peace, then let us die in peace,' shouted Jones as his followers cheered. When they were silent he said: 'Take the potion like they used to in ancient Greece. It is a revolutionary act ... There is no way we can survive.'

A huge vat was brought in as at every 'white night rehearsal'. Hardly anyone faltered as they stepped forward for their drink.

Jones's empty throne overlooks the carnage of the 'white night'. Beneath the throne, a voice-activated tape-recorder took down all that happened on that appalling night.

SCIENTOLOGY

'We are the heralds of a New Age. Scientology is a passport to this new time.'

Saint Hill Manor, a Georgian manor house near East Grinstead, Sussex. Once the home of the Maharaj of Jaipur, it is now the planetary headquarters of the Church of Scientology.

Founded in the early 1950s, the Church of Scientology is one of the most controversial of modern faiths. It claims to increase a person's intellectual ability and knowledge of himself through psychotherapy.

The church, which has about 2 million members, has been in the newspapers many times. It claims to have been the target for a long-running Nazi conspiracy by the CIA, the FBI, the US Inland Revenue Service and the psychiatric profession, known as the 'Tenyaka Memorial'.

The church has about 65 full-time researchers working to substantiate this claim. In the course of their investigations, they have uncovered many stories which have embarrassed governments. These include drug abuse in prisons, the use of dangerous chemicals as weedkillers, and British involvement in American mind-control experiments.

L. Ron Hubbard

Lafayette Ron Hubbard was born in Nebraska in 1911. He claims that after serving in the US Navy for five years in World War II, he was crippled, blinded and had twice been declared dead by doctors. His restoration to health, he says, was by the principles of 'Dianetics'.

After the war, Hubbard became a well-known science-fiction writer and began developing his theory. In 1950 his 435-page book *Dianetics: The Modern Science of Mental Health* became an overnight best-seller. The book was a sort of do-it-yourself psychoanalysis manual. Hubbard went on to set up dianetic organizations around America, but bankruptcy proceedings and criticisms from medical experts closed the institutes.

Because freedom of religion is guaranteed under the American constitution, Hubbard developed his science into a religion. Since then it has grown worldwide.

The religion of Scientology

Scientologists hold services every Sunday, with robed ministers leading. There are no prayers, and no references to God. The sermon is usually a taped lecture by Ron Hubbard. Scientology also has its own rites of baptism, marriage and funerals.

Hubbard himself claims to have visited heaven on two occasions. On his first visit he found 'the gates ... well done, well built. An avenue of statues of saints leads up to them. The gate pillars are surmounted by marble angels. The entering grounds are very well kept, laid out like the Bush Gardens in Pasadena, so often seen in movies'. But on his second visit, eons later, the place had deteriorated.

Scientology hits the headlines

Scientology has been in the news many times.

In 1963 the US Food and Drug Administration

Ron Hubbard occasionally lectures to his followers. His early interests as a writer of science-fiction have carried over into his new religion, with its mixture of psychiatric ideas, scientific equipment and religious statements.

THE NATURE OF MAN

Scientology teaches that man consists of four parts.

A thetan (pronounced 'thaytan') This is the immortal spirit, which is capable of reincarnation. It is in complete control of the total person and is capable of showing enormous powers. Thetans created the universe, but over millions of years became ensnared in their creation and forgot their true status. It is through Scientology that a thetan becomes aware once again of its potential.

A physical body The thetan enters the physical body at conception.

The analytic mind (conscious) Under normal circumstances this causes the person to act normally.

The reactive mind (subconscious) Injury, shock or pain can cause the analytic mind to switch off. When this happens the reactive mind takes over, recording unpleasant experiences, 'engrams', which occasionally reassert themselves later in life as 'aberrations'—neuroses and other psychological disorders.

When a thetan enters a body it brings with it all the engrams from its millions of years of evolution.

THE WAY TO BE SAVED

According to Hubbard the basis of life is to survive. Scientology provides the means to do this.

A pre-clear This is the term for anyone who still has engrams within him.

A clear To be a clear is the aim of all Scientologists. Those who 'reach clear' will obtain IQs of more than 135, creative vitality, deep relaxation and revitalized memory. There are seven grades to reach clear, achieved through a series of progressive courses, each of which costs more than the previous one. There are then a further eight grades—Operating Thetan 1–8.

Auditor or private counsellor A pre-clear's first step to becoming a clear is through sessions with an auditor. These sessions are a mixture of the confession box and the psychiatrist's couch. The aim is that the pre-clear should confront and overcome the sensitive areas within him.

E-meter or electropsychometer To help the auditor the pre-clear holds an E-meter, a kind of lie detector which monitors stress.

raided the movement's headquarters in Washington and a prosecution followed.

In 1965 an Australian Board of Enquiry into the group produced a report flatly condemning it.

In 1967 the British Minister of Health, Mr Kenneth Robinson, attacked Scientology in the House of Commons. He said: 'It alienates members of families from each other and attributes squalid and disgraceful motives to all who oppose it; its authoritarian principles and practice are a potential menace to the personality and well-being of those so deluded as to become its followers; above all its methods can be a serious danger to the health of those who submit to them.' He then announced sweeping restrictions on the entry of Scientologists into Britain.

Also in 1967 the US Court of Claims ruled that Scientology failed to qualify as a group 'organized and operated entirely for religious purposes'. It then lost its tax-exemption status.

In 1977 the FBI seized documents from the movement's American headquarters. Among other things, these revealed the extraordinary activities of their 'internal intelligence organization'. The organization had harassed a critical author, Paulette Cooper, to enormous lengths, including suing her 14 times, putting her name on pornographic mailing lists and framing her on a charge of bombing.

SCIENTOLOGY AND CHRISTIANITY

Scientology	Christianity
Man is basically good. The cause of all his problems lies in past experiences.	Man is made in the image of God, but has gone his own way rather than God's and so has a bias towards evil.
With the aid of Scientology alone, all man's problems can be put right.	Because of his state of sinfulness, man cannot know God except through Christ, who died for his sin.
Salvation can come only through the expensive counselling sessions of Scientology.	Salvation is a free gift from God, offered to all.
God is irrelevant—only Scientology is of importance.	God is of supreme relevance. The way to him is by Jesus Christ alone.

THE WAY

*'I have read every commentary in existence.
I commit every one
of them to Gehenna.'*

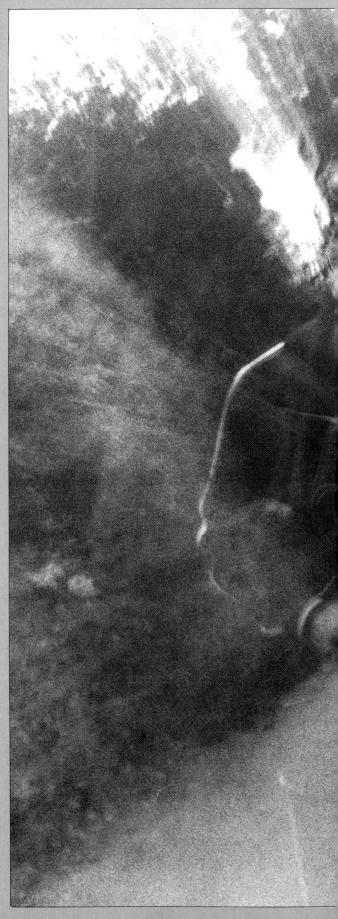

'You can have whatever you want. Every problem you ever had can be overcome when you are fully and accurately instructed' claims the poster around the colleges and universities.

The way to achieve this is to pay $100 and 'join the most amazing class in the world'—The Power for Abundant Living. One course in the USA consists of listening to 33 hours of tapes over a three-week period, and at any one time more than 1,000 Americans are following it.

The initial Bible course promises that 'right' believing will keep away sickness, ensure prosperity and even protect soldiers from enemy bullets.

The course was developed by Victor Paul Wierwille, the founder of The Way International, a Bible research and teaching organization. Wierwille, said by his followers to be the greatest teacher since Paul, claims to have rediscovered the 'true' teachings of the original apostles, which he has since taught to his 23,000 followers in 37 countries.

The start of the Way

Victor Wierwille was born in 1916. He holds a master's degree and a doctorate in theology from an alleged 'degree mill', Pike's Peak Theological Seminary and for a time was a minister in the Evangelical and Reformed Church. But it was in 1942 that he claimed that God spoke to him with a message which provided the answer to his long search for 'the key to powerful, victorious living'.

He claimed that God promised to 'teach me the word as it had not been known since the first century, if I would teach it to others'.

He began his teaching in 1953 and his years of Bible study and his alleged experiences were enough to convince followers that his teaching was right. The teaching puts strong emphasis on the inerrancy of the Bible, so long as it is 'rightly divided'—which Wierwille alone can do. His spoken and written teaching is absolutely authoritative.

His family farm near New Knoxville, Ohio, is the international headquarters of the movement, whose magazine *The Way* now has a circulation of 10,000.

Their Way

The Way's organization is described in the terms

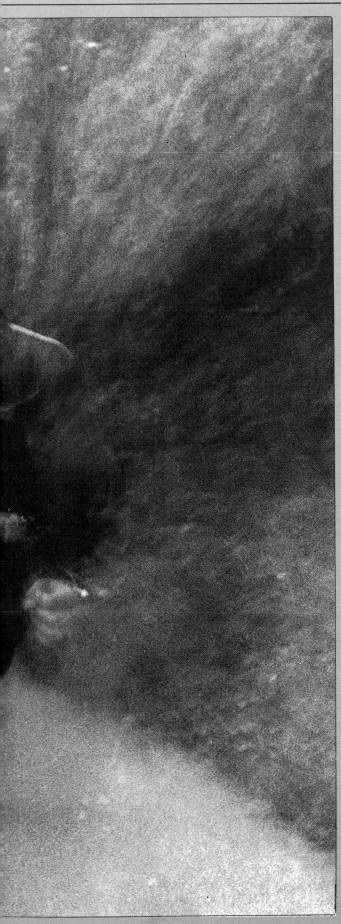

Fitness is vital for followers of the Way. At The Way College, in Emporia, Kansas, exercises form a regular part of daily activity.

But more unusual was a course run for all the students in 1978—the use of military weapons. A pamphlet circulated at the time said that the movement was willing to 'take to the streets with rifles if religious freedom is threatened'.

of a tree. A *twig* is a fellowship group; several fellowships make up a *branch* or city unit; each state unit is a *limb*; limb leaders report back to Regional Directors who report in turn to the International Co-ordinator in Ohio headquarters.

After a new member has taken the foundation class of the Power for Abundant Living there then follows the Intermediate Class and the Advanced Class.

The next stage is to become a WOW Ambassador (Word over the World). Ambassadors take up a part-time job and spend a minimum of eight hours a day witnessing, helping set up local fellowships and running Power for Abundant Living courses.

Finally WOW Ambassadors are encouraged to enrol in The Way Corps, a full-time three-year leadership training programme.

Time

Marie Leonetti was a member of The Way for 22 months before she left the movement. In her story in *Youth Brainwashing and the Extreme Cults* by Ronald Enroth, she said each member of The Way Corps had to keep a record of how he or she spent every minute of the day. They were each given a 'Redeemed Time Analysis' form containing a column entitled 'How I spent my time' and another one 'How I can improve'. There was space opposite every hour from 5 a.m. until midnight.

IS IT THE WAY TO GOD?

The Way believes	The Christian Church believes
The Bible is not the Word of God but only contains the word of God.	'All Scripture is inspired by God' (2 Timothy 3:16).
Jesus is not God. He was a Judean man conceived by God, whose perfect life made him the perfect sacrifice for man.	'In the beginning was the Word (Jesus), and the Word was with God and the Word was God' (John 1:1).
Jesus was crucified with four thieves on a Wednesday.	'And with him they crucified two robbers' (Mark 15:27). This happened on Good Friday.
The Holy Spirit is not personal but merely a 'power from on high'.	'But the Counsellor, the Holy Spirit, whom the Father will send in my name, he will teach you all things' (John 14:26).
The Old Testament and the Gospels are of no use for Christians today. Only the New Testament epistles are.	'All Scripture is inspired by God and profitable for teaching, for reproof, for correcting and for training in righteousness' (2 Timothy 3:16).

THE WORLDWIDE CHURCH OF GOD

A free glossy, monthly magazine with the title 'The Plain Truth' introduces many people to one of the most efficiently run religious organizations of today.

The founder of the Worldwide Church of God is Herbert W. Armstrong, a former sales and advertising executive, who says that just as Jesus chose the highly-educated Paul to take the gospel to the Gentiles, so God has chosen him to spread the gospel in the last days.

Herbert W. Armstrong

As a teenager, Herbert W. Armstrong said he wanted to be rich, famous and learned. By the time he was 40 he had failed with three business ventures.

And Armstrong, born in Des Moines, Iowa, in 1892, was not much more successful with religion after his 'conversion' in 1927 through his wife.

After earlier links with the Quakers and Methodism he became an ordained minister in the Church of God (Seventh Day). But he was asked to leave because of his sensational writings on prophecy and his criticism of other ministers.

When he was 41 he started his own denomination. He began giving lectures on the biblical formula for success and prosperity, which he himself was beginning to enjoy.

He began broadcasting from a local radio station and printing a paper to give to interested listeners. The movement expanded rapidly and in 1968 the Radio Church of God became the Worldwide Church of God. At its peak in 1973, 3.2 million copies of *The Plain Truth* were distributed, and *The World Tomorrow* was broadcast on more than 400 radio and TV stations. More recently, *Quest* magazine has been distributed in America and Great Britain. With its glossy production and its aim of 'the pursuit of excellence' it has reached many readers.

Is it the Plain Truth?

Since 1973, controversies have hit the Worldwide Church of God. In 1972 Garner Ted Armstrong, the founder's son and heir, was relieved of his duties with the radio and as vice-president of the organization and vice-chancellor of the three-college campus. He went on indefinite leave of absence 'for purely personal reasons'. He returned four months later but only to his radio work. Rumours of sexual misdemeanours began circulating.

In February 1974 six ministers resigned from the church over Garner Armstrong's alleged

Armstrong's message is a mixture of religion and personal development. This illustration is part of an advertisement for his booklet *The Seven Laws of Success*.

Members of the church are called to be ambassadors of the message.

The emphasis is on witnessing to others, not trying to convert them. One way is by education and so Armstrong has set up his own radio programmes and three 'ambassador colleges' in America, Australia and England.

sexual misconduct. In all, 29 ministers and 2,000 members joined a rival church, The Associated Church of God. Garner Armstrong has now left the movement. Further splits have since taken place.

A 92-page exposé, which had taken two years to prepare, was published in 1977 by six ex-students

According to *Plain Truth*, the prophet Jeremiah escorted the last king of Judah's daughter to Ireland in 569 BC and carried with him the stone which Jacob had used as a pillow when he had the dream of a ladder between heaven and earth (Genesis 28). Today that stone, says the magazine, is under the Coronation Chair in Westminster Abbey—the Stone of Scone.

PROPHECY

Prophecy is an important part of Armstrong's message, which includes the following teaching.

● The Romans successfully stamped out the preaching of the gospel in AD 69 when Jerusalem fell. A counterfeit gospel was preached until the true church appeared again on the first Sunday of 1934. This was the day when *The World Tomorrow* began broadcasting and *The Plain Truth* was first published.

● The 'ten lost tribes of Israel' wandered across Europe after being freed from their captivity in Assyria. They were the forefathers of the British people. Proof of this, says Armstrong, is the word 'Saxon', which is derived from 'Isaac's son'. Similarly 'Denmark' comes from 'Dan's Mark'.

● The return of the Jews to Israel indicates that the temple will soon be rebuilt as prophesied in the Old Testament. It has been claimed that a young Australian who tried to burn down Jerusalem's Al Aksa Mosque so that the temple could be rebuilt was a member of the Church.

KEY BELIEFS

● God is a family, a team made up of resurrected believers.

● The purpose of life is that God is reproducing himself in us. At the resurrection we shall be changed instantly from mortal to immortal. We shall then be like God, part of his family.

● Before Jesus was conceived by Mary he was not the Son of God.

● Everyone can get to heaven, but only if they keep all the commandments, as interpreted by Armstrong.

● When Jesus returns to earth he will offer salvation to everyone. Those who died without learning about Christ will be given a second chance as they will be resurrected during a 100-year period after Jesus' 1,000-year reign on earth.

● The Holy Spirit is not personal— but 'a divine, spiritual love'.

● Sickness is the penalty for sin. Healing is forgiveness. God is the only real physician.

● The 'end of the age' will come soon, with wars, famines and disasters. Christ will bring these to an end and set up his kingdom. The 12 tribes of Israel will be reunited and will keep all God's laws, as an example to the rest of the world.

LIFESTYLE

Members of the Worldwide Church of God live according to strict rules.

● They must keep to the Old Testament laws and calendar of feasts. New Testament festivals such as Easter and Whitsuntide are considered as pagan. Christmas parties and birthdays are not celebrated.

● At all the major Jewish festivals special offerings are made to the church. These, on top of regular offerings, bring their giving to over 20 per cent of their income.

● They must join a congregation, which will meet in a hall. A typical service will include a sermon, hymn-singing, Bible teaching and reports on the group's work.

● They must be baptized as adults.

● They must take the Lord's Supper once a year, at Passover.

● They must eat food according to the strict Jewish laws.

● They must keep Saturday as the Sabbath.

of the Ambassador College. Their complaints against the Worldwide Church of God included financial irregularities, exploitation of members, opulence and false prophecies. (Armstrong prophesied three dates for Christ's return to earth, all of which have passed.)

BAHA'I

Leo Tolstoy described it as 'the highest and purest form of religious teaching'. Historian Arnold Toynbee has predicted that it will be 'the world religion of the future'.

In 1960 in America there were just 10,000 followers of the Baha'i Faith, a religion one century old. Within 10 years that figure had soared to 100,000 and today Baha'i is one of the world's fastest-growing religious groups.

Baha'is believe that a wealthy Iranian, Baha'u'llah was the manifestation of God for this day and age. Baha'i teaches that all religions are basically one and the same. It emphasizes the oneness of mankind, peace, universal justice and racial harmony.

The forerunner

The origin of Baha'i dates back to 23 May 1844. Mulla Husayn was a young visitor to the Iranian town of Shiraz. He was a member of the devout Muslim Shaykhi sect, who believed that a divine messenger was about to be sent into the world.

In Shiraz, Husayn met a young Iranian, who took him home. 'How will you recognize the messenger?' asked his host, Siyyid Ali-Muhammad.

'He will be between 20 and 30, medium height, won't smoke, will have no physical defects, will possess great knowledge and be descended from Fatimih, the daughter of Muhammad.'

'I am he,' replied the host: from that time on he was known as the Bab, the gate.

Since then every year on 23 May, Baha'is have celebrated the Anniversary of the Declaration of the Bab, when God showed himself to his people through this forerunner, who heralded their coming great Messiah.

The founder

The Bab spent three of the next six years in prison, before being shot in Tabriz in 1850. During that time, 10,000 of his followers were martyred and many thousands more were imprisoned.

One of these was a wealthy nobleman, Mirza Husayn Ali. Whilst he was in jail, he claimed that in a vision, God called him to announce to the world the coming of the Promised One. Four years earlier, he had assumed a new name, Baha'u'llah, 'the glory and splendour of God'. On his release he was exiled to Baghdad where he began to reveal the Baha'i scriptures. But he did not announce publicly that he was the Promised One until 1863. Baha'u'llah's half-brother had tried to start a

In 1850 the Bab was executed in Tabriz. The execution was surrounded by apparently miraculous events. Years later, Baha'u'llah arranged for the remains of the Bab's body to be brought to Haifa. The beautiful Shrine of the Bab has now become a central point of the Baha'i world.

Baha'u'llah spent much of his life in exile or in prison. At Acre he was held in this prison for nine years. Finally the authorities recognized his innocence and allowed him to leave the prison and live in comfort in the city.

Abdul Baha was one of Baha'u'llah's closest companions. He helped his father in much of his work, and was finally appointed his successor. He achieved much in organizing the new faith of Baha'i.

religious war to oust him from power, and now the Turkish government decided to exile them both.

The interpreter

Baha'u'llah was sent to Constantinople and then to Adrianople. In 1868 he began writing to world leaders with his ideas. The same year he was exiled once more.

Baha'u'llah spent the rest of his life in Acre, near Haifa in Palestine, where he was allowed to live freely and in comfort. After his death in 1892 his son, Abbas Effendi, was appointed to control the movement and took the title Abdul Baha, 'the servant of Baha'. Today Haifa is the administrative centre of the faith.

KEY TEACHING

The Oneness of God God is one and there is one God for all the world.

The oneness of religion All the great religions came originally from God revealed through his messengers. They are all fulfilled in the Baha'i faith.

The oneness of man Everyone belongs to the same human family. 'The earth is but one country and mankind its citizens' (Baha'u'llah).

Equality All prejudices of colour, nation, creed and class are destructive and must be abandoned.

Education All children must have the chance of education.

Equality of the sexes Man and woman are equal. They are the 'two wings' of humanity. 'Unless both wings are strong and impelled by some common force, the bird (of humanity) cannot fly heavenward.'

Unity of truth Both religion and science are aspects of truth and cannot contradict each other.

A world auxiliary language To help communication and to eliminate misunderstanding every child should be taught, as well as his own language, one other language—the same for all the world.

A world Parliament Elected representatives from every country should have the power to enforce peace where necessary.

These children are learning the history of Baha'i by acting it out.

Lifestyle

Baha'i has no clergy and no religious ritual. Worship of God is by prayer, spiritual reading and the dedication of daily life. Work, too, is seen as a religious offering when performed in a spirit of service.

Followers of the faith live according to the laws of their countries. They may try to get unjust laws altered, but must not become involved in political dissension. One unique part of Baha'i's lifestyle is their calendar, which has 19 months, each of 19 days.

The supreme legislative and governing body of the faith is the Universal House of Justice at the Baha'i World Centre in Haifa, Israel. Local, national and international administrative bodies, the 'Spiritual Assemblies', are elected by the followers and answerable to God alone.

In personal life, followers have a high moral code. They will not gamble, gossip, take drugs or drink alcohol. And they consider marriage to be a life-long spiritual and physical union.

Meetings and conventions are an important way for Bahai's to learn more about their faith.

In 1978 more than 500 Baha'i delegates came from all over the world to an international convention in Haifa.

BAHA'I AND CHRISTIANITY

Baha'i claims to be the fulfilment of Christianity, but in several points the two differ.

Baha'i teaches that there have been a number of manifestations of God to man. Each manifestation brought the fullest revelation which the people of their time could understand.

Jesus' message was appropriate for his time, and he died in order that men might live. Baha'u'llah was essentially the same manifestation as Jesus. Since he came later, his message was fuller, revealing that all religions have a common origin. He was imprisoned in order that men might be free.

Christian believe that this contradicts the Bible's teaching that Jesus was the unique Son of God. Christians also doubt the idea that mankind's spiritual awareness is increasing. Baha'i teaches that error is in need of guidance, darkness needs light, and falsehood is the lack of truthfulness. It admits the fact of evil, but does not supply the same answer as Christianity. The Bible states bluntly that 'all have sinned and fall short of the glory of God,' and teaches that there is salvation in no one other than Jesus.

So to the Christian, Baha'i is seen as unnecessary. Through his death and resurrection Jesus provides the radical solution to man's need today. 'Christ offered one sacrifice for sins, an offering that is effective for ever' (Hebrews 10:12).

In New Delhi a new Baha'i House of Worship is being built in the shape of a lotus flower. No rituals or ceremonies take place in the Houses of Worship. They are places for quiet contemplation, as Baha'is believe that every person is responsible for their own spiritual development. Every House of Worship has nine sides, since to Baha'is the number nine symbolizes 'open to all'.

FREEMASONRY

It is an all-male friendly society 'founded on the purest principles of piety and virtue,' yet even today it is banned in a quarter of the world.

In the Middle Ages, skilled stonemasons travelled throughout Europe to work on many huge building projects. Their 'trades unions' were the origins of Freemasonry.

As time went by, Freemasonry stopped being a society for masons alone. Symbols and mystical ideas were borrowed from Ancient Egyptian mythology and the movement became a social society.

The ceremony shows an apprentice being admitted into a French Freemasons' Lodge.

Freemasonry is the largest international secret society in the world, with more than 6,000,000 members. It is known for its strange initiation ceremony and its secret signs and handshakes by which members recognize each other. It is claimed that 'no outsider reading the printed rituals can grasp the spirit of Masonry. What at first appears to be childish games can within the atmosphere of the lodge (where Freemasons meet) form a unique bond between men.'

It is an all-male friendly society for mutual help in times of need. Its principles are explained as 'brotherly love, relief and truth'. In theory any believer in God, Christian, Jewish, Muslim, Hindu or Buddhist can become a Freemason.

Members have suffered imprisonment and persecution because Masonry is claimed to be anti-patriotic and anti-Christian. Even today Freemasonry is banned in Russia, China, Hungary, Spain and Portugal. Many of the major Christian bodies including the Salvation Army and the Roman Catholic and Greek Orthodox churches forbid their members to become masons. But in the Church of England and the Free Churches there is no ban and leading members of these churches have held high office in Freemasonry.

In many ways, Freemasonry acts as a businessman's guild. There is strong emphasis on giving to charities—some of which, such as Masonic hospitals and schools, are of great help to Masons. And in the past Masonry has been the passport to success in the world of finance, law and, surprisingly, licensed victualling!

Some of the signs and symbols of Freemasonry.

How it began

During the Middle Ages all crafts had their secret skills and passwords in order that their members could keep the limited amount of work available to themselves and stop other people cashing in.

One group of craftsmen were the freemasons who travelled freely from country to country helping build cathedrals and churches. Near their sites and temporary homes they built 'lodges' where they could spend their leisure hours together.

As cathedral building began to decline so freemasons began accepting honorary members to boost their numbers.

During the seventeenth century working masons began to drop the 'free' prefix, while 'speculative' members took the title 'free and accepted' and began adopting the rites and trappings of ancient religious orders.

In 1717 the first Grand Lodge was founded in England. In 1725 a group of English noblemen staying in Paris founded a lodge there and soon Freemasonry spread throughout Europe.

One important member was Count Cagliostro (1743–95) who claimed to make gold, cause miracle cures, prolong sexual powers and extend life to 5,557 years. He dominated the Lyon Lodge and created his own brand of 'Egyptian Masonry' which included women's lodges presided over by a 'Queen of Sheba'.

Persecution

Freemasonry met much opposition and many members were imprisoned. In 1737 Louis XV of France issued an edict forbidding all loyal subjects to have anything to do with the movement, while in 1738 Pope Clement XII issued a Papal bull forbidding Catholics from joining Freemasonry with the threat of excommunication. He said they were 'depraved and perverted' and most 'suspect of heresy'.

Since then Freemasons have been blamed for the French Revolution, the First World War, Germany's runaway inflation of 1924 and the Spanish Civil War. But since the Second World War when Freemasons fought in the resistance movements, the anti-patriotism jibe and the attacks by the church have become much less frequent.

FREEMASONRY

To be a Freemason one has to be an adult male believing in the existence of a supreme being and the immortality of the soul—and be able to pay the subscription. Members cannot ask to join; hints are usually dropped that they would be welcome if they wished to join.

The actual initiation ceremony is very dramatic and full of symbolism.

Stage one. The candidate takes off his jacket and tie and removes any money or metal items to show he has entered the Freemasons 'poor and penniless'. His left trouser leg is then rolled up to his knee, his shirt is opened to expose his left breast and his right shoe is removed and replaced by a slipper. He is blindfolded to show 'his state of darkness' and a running noose or 'cable-tow' is placed round his neck.

Stage two. He is led to the lodge threshold where his way is barred by the Inner Guard who holds a pointed dagger to his bare chest.

Stage three. He is then led to the Worshipful Master, the chief officer of the lodge. Kneeling before him he answers a series of ritual questions before swearing an oath of secrecy.

Should he divulge any of the Masonic secrets he accepts the penalties of 'having my throat cut across, my tongue torn out by the root, and buried in the sand', although this is seen as symbolic. Or he may be 'branded as a wilfully perjured individual void of all moral worth and totally unfit to be received into this worshipful Lodge'.

Stage four. The candidate has now entered into the light of masonry. The blindfold and the noose are removed and he is given the step, the sign, the grip and the word of an entered Apprentice Freemason. He is also presented with the following objects: a 24-inch gauge representing the 24 hours of the day to be spent in work, prayer and refreshment, a gavel or hammer representing the force of conscience and a chisel showing the advantage of education. Finally he is encouraged to obey the laws of Freemasonry, the Bible and the state.

When the ceremony is over the candidate has 'worked the first degreè' and within a few months may attain the two 'Craft' degrees of Fellow-Craft and Master Mason.

CAN A CHRISTIAN BE A FREEMASON?

Freemasonry claims to be acceptable to all religions. But its teachings include many points which Christians are hard put to agree with.

● The 'lost name of God' is the underlying object in all Masonic Ritual. In the initiation ceremony the candidate is introduced to God as the 'GAOTU', the Grand Architect of the Universe. As a fellow craft member he is taught a further name JHVH—short for Jehovah. As a Master Mason he learns there is far more about the mystic name which is revealed in the Royal Arch Degree. The mystic name is discovered to be a combination of Jewish and Middle-Eastern names of God, which is never pronounced except by three Royal Arch masons each saying one syllable.

● Freemasons have many gods who are considered equal to Jesus.

● Masonic literature denies that Jesus is the only saviour of the world.

● Freemasons reject Christ's death on the cross as God's sole remedy for sin.

● Salvation depends on works, not faith in God.

● The sacred books of many religions, such as the Vedas and Koran, are regarded equally as revelations from God.

● At the initiation ceremony the candidate has to confess he is in darkness reaching for the light. A Christian believes he has found the true light; Jesus said: 'I am the light of the world' (John 8:12).

MORAL RE-ARMAMENT

When man listens, God speaks; when man obeys, God acts; when God acts, nations change.

Moral Re-Armament looks forward to a God-controlled world. Followers believe they can change the world by changing individuals through 'soul surgery'.

Founded by an American, Frank D.N. Buchman, around 1920, it has been known by many names including The Oxford Group, Buchmanism, The New Groupers and the First Century Christian Fellowship. It changed its name to Moral Re-Armament in 1938 to honour its leader's 60th birthday. With the threat of war and the talk of re-armament against Germany as the theme of the time, Buchman said that what the world needed was moral re-armament.

Frank Buchman

Buchman was born in Pennsburg, Pennsylvania, in 1878 and ordained a Lutheran pastor in 1902.

On a visit to Keswick, in England, he heard a woman preaching about the way Jesus' death on the cross had changed her life. At the time Buchman was very depressed, having just resigned after a disagreement with six trustees of a boys' hostel.

Hearing the woman led to a radical conversion for Buchman. He wrote a letter of apology to the six trustees and the relationships were mended. On his return to America he became chaplain at Pennsylvania State College. He began to develop the principles of Moral Re-Armament, arguing that religion was not essentially a matter of intellect or emotions but of the will.

Two Anglican clergy invited him to Oxford and Cambridge to talk to the students and in 1921 he formed the Oxford Group, largely consisting of students. The movement spread rapidly to

The basic message of Moral Re-Armament is simple.

One way in which Moral Re-Armament puts over its ideas to the world is through films and plays. The Westminster Theatre in London is owned by the movement.

Another important work is the organization of houseparties, where people can relax and enjoy each other's company and share their personal testimonies and the confession of their sins. The first such houseparty was in 1918 in Kuling, China.

THE PRINCIPLES OF MORAL RE-ARMAMENT

Moral Re-Armament has no creed and instead of members it draws sponsors. To bring about a change in their life sponsors go through five stages, the five Cs.

Conviction: realizing their sins.
Contrition: being sorry.
Confession: saying sorry.

Conversion: living a new life.
Continuance: continuing to live that new life.

Once a member's life has been changed he should strive for the four absolutes in his life,

absolute honesty
absolute purity

absolute unselfishness
absolute love.

These virtues are to be attained by the four principles:

Sharing The confession of sins and temptations is used as a witness to help others recognize and acknowledge their own sins.
Surrendering Past, present and future life is surrendered to God's keeping and direction.

Restitution This involves paying back to all whom one has wronged directly or indirectly.
Guidance This means listening to, accepting, relying on God's guidance and carrying it out in everything one does or says, great or small.

Holland in 1927, South Africa in 1928, Canada in 1932 and Scandinavia in 1938. By the time Buchman died in 1961 the movement was worldwide.

The movement has no specific membership—men and women are loosely associated with it. They strive to live according to the 'four absolutes', to listen to God frequently in times of quiet during the day and to follow what God tells them.

Christians and Moral Re-Armament

Though many Christians have been involved in the movement, Moral Re-Armament is not specifically Christian. Indeed, it embraces people of all faiths.

The strong points of Moral Re-Armament include the importance placed on changed lives and on witnessing to others, and the obvious effort which has been put into solving political and industrial problems. Many politicians and industrial leaders have spoken together on the independent and friendly platform of Moral Re-Armament. In the years after the Second World War the movement was active in helping the reconciliation between France and Germany.

The movement has been criticized for being snobbish, and concentrating on the influential 'up-and-outs' rather than the down-and-outs. Most important, the movement emphasizes man's own ability to change himself, thereby devaluing God's role in salvation. Christians believe that man can do nothing to save himself, but must look to God alone in Christ if he is to be saved. And guidance for the Christian life comes not from within oneself but from the Word of God, the Bible.

THE RASTAFARIANS

They are the 'cult of the outcasts', the modern-day Israelites in captivity in 'Babylon'–the Jamaican state, the West and all organized institutions.

'Love Jah and live. Hate him and die' says the graffiti. It is written by the Rastamen who believe that Ras Tafari, later crowned Haile Selassie of Ethiopia, is the new Messiah for the black people of the world. 'Jah' is their word for God.

There are more than 7,000 Rastafarians in Jamaica, the home of the movement, and many more in areas of the big cities of England and America where the 'cult of the outcasts' is growing rapidly.

Rastafarians are unmistakable with their hair in long braids, called 'dreadlocks', worn with a woollen hat in the Ethiopian colours of red, black, green and gold.

As they refuse to give up smoking marijuana or to cut their hair (they quote verses from the Bible to back up their arguments), Rastamen have great difficulty in getting jobs and many remain unemployed. Rastamen say they are peaceful, but fringe followers of the cult have sometimes given the faith a violent image.

Followers of Rastafarianism or Ethiopianism deliberately speak a patois to confuse outsiders.

<u>LIFESTYLE</u>

Drink Many Rastafarians refuse to drink because they say that white men enslaved black men by getting them drunk and putting them on slave ships.

Drugs They often take pot (known as 'ganja', 'weed of wisdom' or the 'holy herb') to help them meditate either on their own or in groups. Ganja is seen as a medical, mental and spiritual food. After smoking, they share and debate the understanding reached during meditation in an act called 'reasoning'.

Food Only Ital (natural) food is eaten. Canned or chemical food or food from scavengers such as pigs and shellfish is never eaten.

Marriage This is looked upon as part of the establishment and therefore sinful. Sexual permissiveness is banned, yet a couple need stay together only as long as they want to.

Morals Rastafarians are highly moralistic—deceit, evil thoughts, lying and stealing are all forbidden.

They have no organized church and no place of worship. But many followers will carry a picture of Haile Selassie wherever they go. Some, too, have a red, black, green and gold shed in their garden as a sort of shrine.

Jamaican reggae star Bob Marley has been the single most important figure in spreading Rastafarian ideology. He has attracted many new members to the movement through his successful concert tours and astronomical record sales in England and America.

Since Marley and his group, the Wailers, many other Rasta-based reggae bands have followed, putting their message over in music.

THE RASTAFARIANS

Roots

Few in the 1920s took much notice of the Jamaican, Marcus Mosiah Garvey, who founded the ill-fated Universal Negro Improvement Association to encourage his countrymen to return to their rightful homeland, Africa.

Even those interested soon forgot his prophecy that a black king would be crowned in Africa who would call negroes home. Garvey retreated humiliated to England where he died in 1940.

But when Ras (Prince) Tafari, who said he was a direct descendant of King Solomon, was crowned Emperor Haile Selassie in 1930, the sceptics began to take notice, particularly when the numerous titles at his crowning ceremony included 'Conquering Lion of Judah', 'King of Kings' and 'Lord of Lords'.

Jamaicans began to search the Bible. Some believed that the Book of Revelation was an allegory about them and their suffering and that Haile Selassie was the Living God. To back their case they quoted such verses as Revelation 19:16, 'On his robe and on his thigh he has a name inscribed, King of Kings and Lords of Lords.' Garvey was now recognized as a hero and the father of black nationalism.

For the blacks who had been moving from island to island in the West Indies in search of a home and work, enduring economic depression and race riots, the idea of an African destiny was very appealing.

Garvey had said that they would leave the West Indies by 1960. In 1959 and on a number of other occasions, up to 15,000 people turned up at Kingston, Jamaica, having been persuaded to buy bogus tickets to the homeland. Not surprisingly the ships they were expecting never turned up.

Some followers then decided to try to improve their lot by getting involved in Jamaican politics. When in the 1970s Premier Michael Manley presented himself as 'Joshua leading the people to the Promised Land' and carrying a rod given him by Haile Selassie, he won his elections easily.

Earlier, in April 1966, their 'Messiah' Haile Selassie himself had visited Jamaica and been given a huge reception. Many refused to believe the news of his death in 1975.

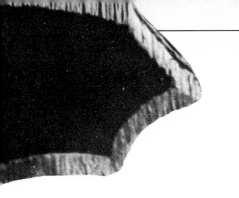

The royal line of Ethiopia is said to be descended from the son of King Solomon and the Queen of Sheba. In 1930, the heir to the throne, Ras Tafari, was crowned Emperor Haile Selassie, and received honours and representations from all over the world. The event provided a vital focus for the aspirations of the black people of the West Indies.

The Jamaican, Mosiah Marcus Garvey, founder of the Universal Negro Improvement Association.

KEY BELIEFS

Many Rastafarians are unclear about the basic beliefs of their religion; some are even unsure who Ras Tafari was. But the central beliefs are as follows:

● God, Jesus, the Israelites and the early Christians were all black. They accuse orthodox Christians of misrepresenting Jesus as a blue-eyed European.

● God became man—not as Jesus but as Haile Selassie, who is still alive and living in another dimension.

● They are the true Jews.

● The Bible was written by and for black people.

● White men are devils.

● Black men will be free only when they are back in Africa.

● Some believe in reincarnation and a few claim to remember their journeys in the slave ships. Others believe that Queen Elizabeth I has been reincarnated as the present Queen of England and that the Duke of Edinburgh is a reincarnation of Philip of Spain.

TRANSCENDENTAL MEDITATION

The Rolling Stones, Mia Farrow, the US army—all of them have investigated the claim of the Maharishi, that his teaching is the ultimate solution to all the problems in the world.

An unknown Indian guru achieved world fame overnight when the Beatles went to see him in 1967. One of them, George, had met the Maharishi Mahesh Yogi when he was studying Indian music and his enthusiasm convinced John, Paul and Ringo to go to a remote corner of Wales to study Transcendental Meditation with the Maharishi.

He says that his system, TM, is not a religion or a philosophy but 'a natural, easy and scientifically verified technique'. There is no dogma to be believed nor need anyone change his or her religion.

More than two and a half million people throughout the world practise TM, including some Christian clergy. Even the US Army has expressed interest in TM.

The practice of TM

The basic technique of TM is simple. Each follower is given a 'mantra', a secret phrase or syllable to fit their personality. Followers are expected to meditate on their mantra for 20 minutes, morning and evening, repeating it over and over again under their breath. Regular meditation, it is claimed, will make them feel more energetic and less tense.

The giving of the mantra takes place in a ceremony called the 'puja'. This is described as a simple Indian ceremony of gratitude for the long tradition of TM. It is performed in Sanskrit and no translation is available to those being initiated.

The Maharishi

Maharishi (meaning Great Sage) Mahesh (his family name) Yogi (one who has achieved union with God) was born Mahesh Prasad Warma in north central India in 1911.

After studying physics at Allahabad University

he graduated when he was 31 and worked in a factory for five years where he began dabbling in yoga in his spare time.

At the end of the Second World War he retreated to the Himalayas to seek enlightenment for 13 years with his guru, Swami Brahmananda Saraswati (Guru Dev). Just before he died Guru Dev told Mahesh Yogi to evolve a single form of meditation for everyone. For two years he stayed in the Himalayas before revealing his ideas to the world in 1959 when he was 48.

He started in Madras but got little response. He then came to London after announcing a nine-year plan to spread his message via the International Meditation Society. The movement was known at this stage as the Spiritual Regeneration Movement. It later changed its name to the Science of Creative Intelligence.

For a while he created little impact in London. But then the Beatles went to see him and suddenly this small Indian in a simple white loincloth and beads, with rubber-thonged sandals and an ever-present flower in his hand, hit the headlines.

But the novelty soon wore off and the Maharishi flew home saying: 'I know I have failed. My mission is over.' He vowed never to return to the West.

But his mission was not over. From his 15-acre, 58-room air-conditioned ashram in Rishikesh, India, he evolved a new plan, aiming to set up 350 teacher training centres which would become universities of TM.

Mentmore Towers in Buckinghamshire, England, the former home of Lord Rosebery and the Rothschilds which the TM movement bought in 1977 for only £248,000.

Maharishi Mahesh Yogi aims to create a 'world government' to administer the 'age of enlightenment' and Mentmore Towers is his 'capital' in Britain.

Here 80 young bachelors look after the house and its 83 acres of land.

Although Mentmore Towers was stripped of its treasures by Sotheby's 'sale of the century' the movement has restocked it with valuable antiques, hung 700 metres of velvet at the windows and even lined the walls with silk.

Since TM began spreading from its headquarters by Lake Lucerne in Switzerland in the early 1970s the movement has bought several mansions in England.

TRANSCENDENTAL MEDITATION

At Mentmore Towers, Lord Rosebery's billiard room has been turned into the Flying Room. With about 70 people aiming to reach heights of up to five feet, a plan has been drawn up to stop anyone bumping into another flyer. The plan divides the room into a parking area, a central reservation, a freeway and a platform area and warns members not to park on the freeway or around the platform. Before TM followers start flying they tick off their names and are reminded of 'flight safety procedures'.

The technique, called the TM-Sidhi programme, is supposed to improve the quality of life not only in the practitioner, but also of the whole community. When sufficient numbers practise TM-Sidhi they 'radiate an influence powerful enough to affect the trends of the whole society'. They believe this will reduce crime rate, accidents and sickness over a wide area.

Is it the way to Creative Intelligence?

There has been opposition to TM in both the East and the West. Some Hindu gurus say the Maharishi has misinterpreted their holy book, the *Bhagavad Gita*. Other yoga and eastern religious authorities dislike his idea of 'instant Nirvana' and his commercialism—would-be followers have to give a week's pay for their courses. Again others reject his linking of TM and materialism.

Some members of TM have left the movement saying they had never learnt to fly despite promises that they would. Instead of peace and tranquillity, their attempts to fly have given them severe mental and physical problems. Meditators of other traditions, such as Christian monks, have long known of these dangers and warned against them. According to some meditators the technique does not solve problems, it merely blurs them. They also say that TM encourages a self-centred approach to life which has harmed their personal relationships.

American psychologist Leon Otis reported that 'a substantial minority' of people meditating for at least 18 months developed anxiety, depression, physical and mental tension and other adverse effects.

IS TM A RELIGION?

● At the puja ceremony no translation of the Sanskrit is given. But the words are in fact a call to Hindu gods asking for help and offering them sacrifices. In particular, Guru Dev is identified as a divine incarnation.

● A mantra is chosen according to a 6,000-year-old tradition, say followers of TM. Actually there are only 16 mantras and the present tradition goes back only to 1973. All the mantras are the names of, or close to the names of, Hindu gods.

● Maharishi is a Hindu bhakti monk and evolved his technique while studying the Hindu Vedic Scriptures.

● Transcendental consciousness is only the first stage of TM. There are four more stages of consciousness ending with 'God consciousness', 'union with God', and 'Brahma consciousness'.

● TM is undoubtedly Hindu in its teachings. Even their basic textbook *The Science of Being and the Art of Living* says TM is the real 'eternal truth' at the base of all religions. Like Hinduism it teaches that God is impersonal; life is a cycle of rebirths; man can become perfect; sin can be overcome through meditation; Jesus Christ was a prophet and not the saviour of the world.

● After a two-year legal battle a federal court in New Jersey ruled that TM is religious by nature. This ruling meant that TM would no longer be taught in state public schools.

GLOSSARY

Many of the ideas of the new faiths take words from existing faiths and give them a different meaning.

In the West, many of the words have been taken from Christianity. So this list not only explains some of the recurring themes of the new faiths, but also brings out the original meaning of the words and their Christian usage.

GOD

Almost all the cults and new faiths have a belief in God, 'Ultimate Reality', 'Universal Truth' or some similar idea.

God Christians believe that there is one God who created and sustains all things. God is not an idea or a force; he is personal. He is characterized by holiness and love. He is separate from his creation. He is one. And he makes himself known to mankind as three different 'persons'; as the Father, as Jesus Christ the 'Son', and as the Holy Spirit.

Jesus Christ A real man who lived in history, Jesus claimed to have come to introduce a whole new world order, which will one day be complete. Many faiths consider him to be a good teacher, a prophet or one of many incarnations of God. Christians believe that Jesus is God himself. By his death for human sin and resurrection to new life, Jesus inaugurated the new age. (See too *The Future*.)

Incarnation God becoming man. Faiths of Eastern origin believe that throughout history, and today, there have been many incarnations. Christians believe that there is one God who became man once, in the person of Jesus Christ.

Holy Spirit The Hebrew word means 'breath' or 'life'. Many faiths have a belief in a 'life-force' of some sort. Christians believe that the Holy Spirit is personal, the very life of God. When someone first believes in Jesus, he receives the Holy Spirit, who then gives him the power to live out the life of Jesus.

Messiah 'Annointed one', the deliverer awaited by the Jews. The term has also been applied to many people who have claimed to reveal God in a special way and to bring salvation to mankind. Christians believe that Jesus is the one and only Messiah, sent by God. ('Christ' is Greek for 'Messiah'.)

HUMANKIND

Underlying the teaching of every faith is a particular belief about the nature of mankind. The beliefs vary widely, and often provide a key to understanding the rest of the movement's teaching.

Origins Most faiths believe that mankind was made by God. Some believe that the creation and the creator are one and the same. Some believe that the creator is no longer concerned with his creation. Christians believe that each person is made in the 'image' of God, with personality, creativity, love and infinite value.

Good and evil Some faiths believe that there is no such thing as evil. Others believe that at heart people are good—and given the right opportunities each person will become good. Christians believe that God created mankind perfect and in fellowship with himself. But mankind chose the way of independence from God. Separation from God was the inevitable result of this deliberate disobedience, 'the fall'. Pain, death and other evils followed.

Enlightenment Any fresh, inspiring understanding of life could be termed 'enlightenment'. Some groups teach that this is the one real need of mankind Christians believe that more is needed.

Salvation Literally 'being saved'. Many groups believe that it is possible for an individual to be saved by good deeds, enlightenment, or even by marriage. Christians believe that Jesus Christ is the only one who can 'save' us from evil, and from being separated from God. For his death paid the price of man's rebellion.

Resurrection 'Rising again' from death. Resurrection involves the body (or a 'new body'), not just the soul. The resurrection of Jesus (the 'best attested fact of history') proved his claim to inaugurate the new age.